THE 7 ROCKS OF LIFE

THE KEY TO FILLING UP YOUR LIFE CUP

STEVEN MAZZURCO

ISBN: 978-1-64184-097-2 (paperback)

ISBN: 978-1-64184-087-3 (ebook)

Website: stevenmazzurco.com
Instagram: @steven_mazzurco

Made in the USA
Middletown, DE
07 May 2019

DEDICATION

I dedicate this book to anyone out there, who may be hurting or just looking for some guidance in certain areas of life. Maybe you feel you are by yourself in life at times or just need a little push to start using all of your talent. I dedicate this book to you. My gift to you is sharing this book and your gift back to us is seeing you shine more than ever after reading it and applying the SeVen RoCk LiFe!

TABLE OF CONTENTS

INTRODUCTION

Sometimes we wait for the "perfect time" to do something. We wait for the weather to be just right, to be the perfect age, for the ideal time of day or month, etc. I have wanted to write a book for years; in fact, since 19 years old. I've always enjoyed poetry and writing at various times of my life; It allowed me to express how I was feeling at the time. It must be the soft Italian/French side of me that was inherited from my parents. Growing up I also had fantastic teachers in middle school who helped me explore myself and that lead to this talent that comes from my heart. I started writing a book about three times in my life. One time in my dorm room in college when I was 21, another after my career in baseball at 26, but finally at 31 years old I was ready. What's incredible is that this all started on a phone and on a plane just writing and journaling things in my life that I was learning and discovering. My thoughts went from my mind to my phone, and now a book to share with the world. Thanks, Steve Jobs, for making a notes section in the iPhone; it came in handy.

What's interesting is that this past year has been the toughest part of my life. Hitting rock bottom in my personal and business life brought me here to write this book as I wrap up one of my hardest trials in life. I have decided to give the world a window into my heart and the lessons that were learned, to help whoever reads this that they may have a breakthrough. Things are looking up now, for which I am grateful, and I'm now able to share what was learned. I have realized the thing you sometimes don't want to do in your life, is what you need to do most to move forward. I felt my heart was called to move me in this direction to share the deepest and lowest points throughout this journey and to use it to help and inspire others to rise up to their full potential. To make a choice, to be on the bench or in the starting lineup in this game called "Life".

We sometimes write or talk about events or circumstances in our life well after they are over, but I believe it's more authentic to share while you are still in the heat of it or wrapping it up because it's current. It's like eating fresh vegetables or basil from the garden. How do I know about that? Because I grew up with an Italian dad who had fresh tomatoes and other vegetables in his garden when I was growing up.

When God blesses you in life, it's your duty to share and be the selfless person who gives back. Life is going to happen *for* each one of us, not just *to* us. I prayed to God to ask what was best for me to do this past year, and so many doors have been opening to pull me in this direction of sharing my life and journey with you all.

INTRODUCTION

"GOD'S GIFT TO YOU IS LIFE. YOUR GIFT TO GOD
IS WHAT YOU DO WITH THAT LIFE."

I promise to be authentic, vulnerable, and honest because that is what you deserve. I am allowing you to read my mail because that's the only way you will know what's in it. We all deserve that. My goal with this book and future projects I do, is one thing—to impact lives. Two things were created during this time, one being the SeVen RoCk LiFe brand (which saved my life) and Project Impact Charities. The goal of these two is simple; to impact lives around the world. To spread love, wisdom, hope, and give funds that people need to make a difference in their communities. We sometimes feel we are not enough to make a difference in this world. We question our self-worth and our ability to create an impact. In reality, we are all worthy of creating greatness.

SeVen RoCk LiFe is a brand with a story that inspires. It's about people living, their everyday lives who are truly inspiring! Whether you're a mom, dad, kid, athlete, entrepreneur, or just someone working hard every day in this game of life, I admire you!

This brand is about three things:

Victorious In Life
Contributor To Society
Fun Along Journey

The "7 Rocks of Life" name came about one day when I was reading a book that was given to me by a friend during my loneliest time of life. I was depressed beyond my imagination and questioning why I was here on earth. My relationship had fallen apart, I lost friendships with people I trusted and cared about; my whole world was turned upside down. Talk about an atomic bomb happening when I thought everything was great. Just a couple of months before that, I was speaking in front of 2,000+ people. Then bam—it happened! From that moment on, a new journey began and things started happening in my life.

Now a great friend, who was once someone look-ing to get into business and mentorship during the beginning of this season of life, gave me a book by Carl Lentz called *Own The Moment*. The first chap-ter asked, "Are you truly available?" I put the book down and said to myself, honestly I haven't been. I wasn't really diving into seeking out the correct knowledge in life. I believed that God was planting a seed, molding me and also pruning some things in my life that needed to change.

But this book is not just about my journey. This is about sharing what I've learned and continue to learn every day. I want to help you get through this time in your life, whether you are struggling with depression, sickness, suicide, drugs, relationships, finances, divorce, or questioning why you're here. Maybe you just need someone to pick you up and say, "You can do it!" I don't claim to be perfect in these seven areas of life, but I will tell you that I've never had more peace and joy, because of focusing on these seven rocks of life.

Life is like a highway, and depending on the weather in your part of the world, potholes will start to form. Imagine you are a car, the road is your life, and the potholes are the adversities you go through as you drive down the highway of life. Your car sometimes hits these potholes, and nothing happens, but over time, you will eventually have a blown tire or axle that makes you pull over. This actually just happened to me where a pothole ruined the rim of my tire and bent the wheel so that air started slowly leaking. The car began to drive oddly because there was less air in the tire. You might see the same thing happen in your life where there's not a sudden and very noticeable blowout, but a slow leak that eventually turns into a flat tire.

Every day can be a battle with the game of life, whether it be the world, jobs, people, or just a battle in our minds that controls us and restricts us from making the progress we desire. I have realized that true joy is a focus, not a feeling. I pray that the journey we go through together in this book gives you insight, wisdom, and perspective in your life in the seven main areas that can give you balance. If you feel broken or lost, don't worry, I have been there. Don't be embarrassed, instead be excited that you are going to be put back together the proper way. I've always heard life is an open book test, but first you must open it. Every book or audio helps increase your understanding. Seeking wisdom is the key to life. It helped me get through my darkest times, and I write this telling you I am still a work in progress. It is a journey that you can always become better no matter what.

Every day is a day to get better, to look in the mirror and say I'm proud of who I am becoming. It's my honor to share this with you. Half of the profits of every book sold will directly fund charities, specific projects, and also missionary work. I've been truly blessed and want to give back, so I created Project Impact Charites, which is about making a difference in people's lives in many ways. I also created a brand called SeVen RoCk LiFe clothing. With every purchase we will be donating another item to a cause we support. We also have a goal to build 100+ schools and playgrounds around the world. Community and environment is key to helping our youth be raised properly. Selfless giving started at a young age for me, ever since my trip to the Dominican Republic to play baseball at 15 years old opened up my eyes to the rest of the world and to see how others are living. I have been blessed with a great business and being able to mentor others, which I started at 20 years old, that has given me a great lifestyle, but it's not just about that. It's about what you leave in people, that help them operate at their full potential. Life trials help you gain perspective on the things that matter. To build a skyscraper, you must have solid bedrock. When you look at New York City, you see an island with tall buildings because the ground is rock solid. If it were sand or another type of soil, it would not be able to hold those buildings or even their subway system. There are seven rocks of life that create a solid foundation so you can build a life that rises to the heights you want and dream of.

In this book, you will learn to be authentic. You will learn to take off the mask we often wear in life. I grew up with plastic covering our couches, and we could never feel what the couch was like underneath.

INTRODUCTION

It is the same thing with us. We sometimes display these avatars that look good externally but are crushed or confused internally. You need to learn how to *own* your identity, not *rent* it, knowing how to be anchored in it so that it doesn't move with the strong currents of life. Sometimes, the only image we have in life is our social media image, and we forget our own true offline image. The one we have to sleep with, walk with, and brush our teeth with. The online image is not always on, but we wake up to our offline image every day. We live two lives: online and offline.

"SOMETIMES WE ARE SMILING IN FRONT OF THE CAMERA BUT DYING BEHIND THE SCENES."

As I wrote this book, I actually deactivated my social media for a couple of months to create clarity in my life. It's created a world of self-discovery and understanding that I cannot describe. I talk about this in the first chapter; you need to build your home instead of living in others' homes your whole life. I think we have a depression, anxiety, and suicide problem in today's world due to self-comparison.

I wrote this book because I felt God's calling in my heart. I've always wanted to write a book but thought that I didn't have enough life experiences to share. I am still learning every day. I pray and hope this book impacts your life and any others with whom you may share it. I heard the following recently. There are two days you leave this earth: the day you pass, and the day your name is said for the last time because you never impacted society or your family to remember your name. It's not what you leave *for* people; it's what you leave *in* people that matters. Throughout this book, I will give the rocks of life that keep you balanced. I know I'm not the only one in this world that goes through life with a smile while inside there is something broken, missing, or not in alignment.

"So what are these 7 rocks?" The seven key rocks of life that have kept me grounded and took me out of my deepest point of life are: *Spiritual, Relationships, Finances, Health, Income Streams, Organization, and Personal Growth.* These are the areas you will learn about. I say this book is an honest cheat code of things I wished I had learned in school growing up.

The following couple is one of the few reasons the Seven Rock Life brand started. One day, the husband went into a bookstore and saw a book called *Never Give Up*. He skimmed through it and decided to buy it for his wife. She started reading it, and then thought about me and decided to send the book to my house not knowing what I was going through. The title hit home, and I started reading it right away. One part changed the course of my life and my perspective on everything.

If your goal is to fill up an empty cup and you have rocks, pebbles, sand, and water, which one goes in first? The rocks, then the pebbles in between, the sand will sink down, and the water will finish it off. If you put the sand or water first, it will overflow and not fit properly. We sometimes make things or people in our life the rocks and put them first when we should be putting them last to fill the cup properly.

INTRODUCTION

I asked myself what the rocks were in my life that create a balanced foundation so that everything fits into my cup of life.

This past year, I learned and discovered so much about life and myself. I want to help you as much as I can in whatever part of the world you are in. I want to help you get through the tough time you may be going through where you may feel alone or confused. Maybe you're just looking to improve upon where you are currently at in your life. I may not know you personally, but I empathize with what you are going through. Together, we will help you get out of this funk. Whether it is a health issue, divorce, finances, depression, purpose, anxiety, or something else, I pray God gives you clarity.

I chose seven rocks because it's a special number that the Bible talks about. There are seven days in a week, which allows you to read a chapter a day to complete this in one week. Also, it's Mickey Mantle's jersey number. He was a pretty good baseball player. Go Yankees!

This book has a challenge for you called The SeVen RoCk LiFe Challenge! For everyone who reads the book in seven days (be honest, God's watching) I will pick seven random winners a month. You will have to post on your story or social media, a picture and your favorite quote in the book that impacted you and also hashtag #SevenRockLife. The winners will get either another book for a friend, clothing from the SeVen RoCk LiFe brand, or get a donation to a charity that you really believe in.

Enjoy *The Seven Rocks of Life*. I'm excited to go on this journey with you. This is about discovering yourself. It's about living a life with a great foundation that will allow you to operate at your full potential. A great life is available to you, and you deserve it. The world needs you in it. You are an important person and have a special purpose. I hope to help you discover that throughout this seven-day journey of reading this book. It's my honor and privilege to share this book with you. I pray God blesses you through this reading and the season of life you are in. My name is Steven Mazzurco, and I am your friend. Enjoy!

1

SPIRITUAL

I was in Miami talking with a friend, and the word SWAG kept coming up. We asked each other what a good acronym for that word was because we didn't know one. He gave me ten minutes to create one, or I had to pay for dinner. I thought about it and came up with this in the ninth minute: Start With Appreciating God.

I grew up going to Bible study, usually crying about having to go there. I'm not sure why, but I think it was during dinnertime and I was always hungry. Going to a Catholic church, I never truly understood what was being spoken about. I only knew about Mary, the Father, the Son, and the Holy Spirit. I drank the grape juice and ate the cracker, not knowing why. But as I was exposed to great people and gained the right wisdom and principles of life, I realized life becomes an open book test if you seek out wisdom. I have heard that "Bible" stands for Basic Instructions Before Leaving Earth. In our world, we really don't want information or content, we only want the truth about life. In this rock, I found the

1

truth that helped me very much. This chapter is the longest because I've learned most of my wisdom on this journey, especially this past year through the highs and lows life gave me. This rock saved my life and got me out of depression. It brought clarity and peace in my life.

BATMAN VS. JOKER

I've come to realize that we all have a little Batman and Joker in us. The question is which one is controlling you more. We sometimes let our flesh make decisions, which is sin. We have our good side and our bad side. If you notice, the joker never killed Batman in the movie, even though he had his chances. What he did do was play mind games and made him question his intentions and who he really was. Every day, we work on being the best version God wants us to be.

You will not be perfect, but it's about growing and pursuing to become a better version that's deep inside of you. Sometimes, our best versions lie dormant, but the challenge is we never water it or place it into an environment where it can prosper. You need certain things, people, or walks of life to help you take it out. It's like having a car with a 500-hp engine that goes 180 mph, but you live in NYC, and the speed limit is 25 mph on roads with potholes. You have all this power but not the right place to drive it and utilize it to its fullest potential. Growing in your spiritual walk will allow you to discover yourself and where you can drive to allow you to use all of your God-given talents.

Throughout our life, God messages us. When you look on your iPhone, you will see where your message from someone texting you is gray, and your messages are blue. Go look now. Sometimes, God asks why our conversation with him is only gray. It's a one-way conversation, and you don't see any blue. That's because we sometimes forget to message back and don't realize He is talking to us, but we are not listening or responding. We are distracted by everything around us and everyone giving us advice instead of the man who made you! We get answers every day, but sometimes we are too distracted by life to see those opportunities arise.

The inner voice in you is about listening to your heart, and with the right people guiding you, realizing that with Him you are in control of acquiring the next better version of you. This is a life-long journey. Your spiritual walk will introduce you to the version that you were destined to be. Sometimes, culture or our environment limits us from becoming that version. I battled every day working toward that, and it's a fight, but deep down inside, we burn truly to want to become better in all areas.

ENLIGHTENED LIFE

We want to live an enlightened life, and there are four elements to be able to do that:

- Forgive yourself
- Surrender
- Utilize the circumstances
- Serve others

Forgiving yourself is key to your mistakes. Failure is the successful discovery of learning something that did not work. You must not forget things, but you must forgive others and yourself, which is necessary for true freedom. When you hold things in, it burns you inside. You learn when things don't go your way to embrace it and forgive yourself for not being perfect. Forgiving others for potential wrongs they have done is a huge part of forgiveness as well. Forgiveness does not change the past, but it will enlarge your future tremendously. It's not just about the person you're forgiving; it's about the new you and what you are now becoming through this process.

Surrendering is definitely something I have struggled with and continue to at times. But I'm working on getting better. A lot of people will say this shows weakness, but it actually shows strength in God's eyes that you are willing to be guided by those with secure maps in life to where you want to go or be. He also wants you to know He has your heart and your mind toward Him. With this type of attitude, blessings come about. From having a personality called choleric and wanting control, I've slowly learned how to give up control at certain times because, in the end, there are always things you can and cannot control. It's like beach erosion. You can put more sand on the beach, but then—wham!—a storm comes and washes it all away. It's something more powerful that takes over what humans tried to do. Traffic is another great example. You can't change it, so just smile.

There is a water park by us called Splish Splash, and when you go down the rides, you have to trust and surrender to where the ride takes you. You try and grab the walls, but the momentum is taking you with the slide. Unfortunately, in the end, you may even get a wedgie, but you just have to accept it and wait till the ride is done. Ha! The more you try to control, the less control you realize you have. Sometimes in life, God is that way. We try to be in control, but at the end of the day, we are not.

Think back to when you were a kid at the supermarket. When you're at a supermarket, and you are a kid driving in the shopping cart in one of those carts that has a seat in the front with a wheel. As a kid, you think you are driving the cart, but it's really your mom that is pushing you. You think you are in control, but again you're not.

Know what God is in control of and what you are in control of. Many times, we try to control others, but that never works. I've been there in my life but finally realized I can't change other people's actions. You need to surrender to the situation and let the universe do its job with whatever is going on. Do your part but understand you can't always take apart the situation. Trust and have faith that the season you're going through will pass in due time. Learn to surrender to the water slides of life.

Utilizing circumstances is being able to make the most of a situation. It's like if you miss a flight or it's canceled. You can choose to get upset or decide that this is the time to call a friend, listen to an audio, read, or talk to a stranger and get to know them. It's being able to have that mindset of the glass half full, not empty. Even as I'm writing this, I'm utilizing my circumstances where I can either be depressed and down, or I can share the knowledge to help others currently experiencing pain to overcome and win this inner self battle. It's crazy to think that through this journey I've learned so much about life, even during the darkest times. Seven months ago, I was at rock bottom, and now feel so blessed and grateful about life. I have learned through this season of life to inspire and teach others through the adversities I have experienced.

Serving others allows you to take your eyes off yourself and stop being self-consumed with your own problems. It gives you perspective and appreciation when you do charities or just go out of your way to help someone who doesn't benefit you. It's being selfless in those times when you want to be selfish. Writing this book was a big fear of the unknown. At the same time, I would feel guilty if I didn't share this information and the truth I continue to learn every day. Even if it impacts and saves just one life, that's all that matters to me. It's like the story of the girl throwing a starfish back into the water that had been on the shore. An old man said there were hundreds of them, so why bother. She said it mattered to that one, and that's all that mattered.

Take that perspective every day you go out there in this world. Become that servant leader and give freely. We've all been told to be careful that we don't get taken advantage of. The truth is that you won't get taken advantage of if you give freely. But if you're giving only to keep count of what people owe you, it will cost you a lot when you don't get anything in return.

I remember giving a month's salary to a friend to fix their car, trusting I would get it back but not expecting it. I gave freely, and what's crazy is that it was just about the time my trial of life started. God was already preparing me and testing me, and I didn't even know. I never got back the money, but that didn't matter. I gave with no expectation and only wanted that person to live a great life. Because of that, they were able to spend the holidays with their kids. God will bless you with abundance in your life, but make sure you don't keep all of it.

"TRULY LEARN TO GIVE YOURSELF UP AT TIMES TO OTHERS WHO NEED IT. IT DOESN'T HAVE TO BE JUST MONEY; IT CAN BE YOUR TIME OR YOUR HEART, WHICH ARE THE MOST EXPENSIVE GIFTS YOU CAN GIVE!"

KISS IT GOODBYE

Whatever your faith is, Buddhism, Christian, Muslim, Jewish, etc., it's those principles they teach you that we need to follow. We sometimes go through life trying to put it together without reading some type of manual, and then we wonder why there are missing parts or extra pieces. We see broken families or relationships because of forgiveness issues, upbringing issues, or generational curses that carry on with us. I grew up in an Italian family, and not seeing certain family growing up and seeing relationships broken made question the reason of that happening.

Sometimes, I feel like it was due to dumb reasons, like someone taking someone's cannoli at a wedding and never asking, so they didn't talk for years. It comes down to things that are little and sad or something like money issues (which is a piece of paper), and that hurts. It's sad sometimes that something as insignificant as money can cut relationships in half. I've seen it in my own life, and I'm sure you have as well. The power of forgiveness is a heart issue. I've learned that from my mentors through challenges they have endured and the true forgiveness they decided to have. When others would not forgive, they did. You don't forgive for yourself; you forgive for your life and future family.

I love this story by Joel Osteen.

Kiss It Goodbye
Post by Joel Osteen on February 15, 2019

In the Scripture, a lady named Naomi and her family had left Bethlehem because of a famine and moved to Moab. Life was good, but then her husband unexpectedly died. She never dreamed she would be a widow. Ten years later, both of her married sons died. She was so heartbroken that she decided to move back to Bethlehem. She told her daughters-in-law, Ruth and Orpah, to go back to their homes and start new lives. Ruth refused to leave Naomi, but Orpah took her advice and went home.

After all Naomi had been through, she could have thought, "Orpah, how can you leave me at my lowest moment? How am I going to make it at my age?" She could have felt betrayed and angry, but that would have kept her from the new things God had in store. Instead the Scripture says she "kissed Orpah goodbye" (Ruth 1:9). Orpah represented the hurts, the disappointments, the broken dreams, and the things Naomi didn't understand. She was saying by her actions, "Life hasn't been fair, but I know that what was meant for my harm, God can turn to my advantage," which is exactly what happened. She and Ruth moved back to Bethlehem where Ruth married a wealthy man named Boaz. They had a baby whom Naomi took care of as though it were her own son. After all the hurt and loss, Naomi said, "I never dreamed I would be this happy and fulfilled." Her latter days were better than her former days. This would have never happened if she had not kissed Orpah goodbye.

When life doesn't turn out the way you thought, remind yourself that God is still in control. If you're going to reach your destiny, you have to learn to kiss negative things goodbye. People may walk away. Life may not turn out the way you had planned. It's tempting to get bitter, hold a grudge, and lose your passion. You have to kiss the bitterness goodbye, kiss the person that left you goodbye, and kiss the dream that didn't work out goodbye.

Sometimes God closes the door. He'll move people out of your life. There are people and opportunities that were assigned to your past that are not assigned to your future. They were right for a season, but that season may come to an end.

The key is how you handle the closed door, how you handle the disappointment, how you handle the person who did you wrong. You can't embrace the new things God has in store as long as you're holding on to the old. Accept it as God's plan, kiss it goodbye, and move on. God knows how to bring you out better than you were before.

LOVE IS LIGHT, HATE IS HEAVY

Recently, I learned about agape love, which is the purest form of love. I won't get into it in detail, but it's truly a hard place to get to. I'll be honest, I battle getting to that place even now, but from where I was to now is totally different from certain situations or things people do or say. I've learned that:

"LOVE IS THE MOST POWERFUL LANGUAGE
IN THE WORLD."

Sometimes, life builds such a callous heart that it becomes broken and hurt. Every day is a battle to live that life of integrity, character, love, and forgiveness. Your spiritual walk is a walk that you need to go on. I knew that God was there for me when the world seemed not to care. I know that some of you reading this feel the same way. When I wanted to give up on my life and call it quits, my relationship with God and my walk with Him helped me grow. You get broken first at times to be built up properly as you rebuild. There is a song by Micah Tyler called "Different" that hit home with me early on in my trial and changed my life. I recommend you go right now and listen to it on YouTube and watch the video as you listen to the lyrics.

> I don't wanna hear anymore, teach me to listen
> I don't wanna see anymore, give me a vision
> That you could move this heart, to be set apart
> I don't need to recognize, the man in the mirror
> And I don't wanna trade Your plan, for something familiar
> I can't waste a day, I can't stay the same
>
> I wanna be different
> I wanna be changed
> 'Til all of me is gone
> And all that remains
> Is a fire so bright
> The whole world can see
> That there's something different
> So come and be different
> In me
>
> And I don't wanna spend my life, stuck in a pattern
> And I don't wanna gain this world but lose what matters
> And so I'm giving up, everything because
>
> I wanna be different
> I wanna be changed
> 'Til all of me is gone
> And all that remains
> Is a fire so bright

The whole world can see
That there's something different
So come and be different;

I know, that I am far, from perfect
But through You, the cross still says, I'm worth it
So take this beating in my heart and
Come and finish what You started
When they see me, let them see You
'Cause I just wanna be different, ye-ey

I wanna be different
I wanna be changed
'Til all of me is gone
And all that remains
Oh is a fire so bright
The whole world can see
That there's something different
So come and be different
I just wanna be different
So could You be different
In me

When I heard that song, I broke down crying because that was exactly how I felt. It is such a beautiful song. It's a struggle at times, though. As you lean into this part of your life, there is a sense of purpose, a peace that starts to come in your life. We often look for approval from so many instead of what our higher power wants in our lives.

That's why we struggle with joy at times. I've come to realize that joy is a focus, not a feeling. When we make it a feeling, it robs us of our happiness, and we experience an emotional roller coaster. We let finances, job issues, and relationship issues starve us from our joy. We go through life moving but not truly enjoying it. It's like driving in an Uber car that has an odor but it's moving to get you to your destination. The challenge is that the odor is terrible, and you're not enjoying the ride. You wish you had that new fresh car scent from the car wash that would stay with you, but you didn't get it. We let the external environment control and manage our internal environment. We become enslaved to what others think of us and what things happen to us. When you expect perfection in everything and everyone, you lose peace and get let down. Stop expecting perfection, and you will gain peace.

At times, we get caught up in this old story that expired in our life. We talk about it and others all the time. We need to create a new story that we start to write. God wants that as well. Learn from that old story, but we must not live it. It's in the past. There is a reason why the rear-view mirror is smaller than the windshield of your car. If you look behind too much, you will lose sight of where you're going and eventually hit something. That's what depression is. When my relationship came crashing down, along with other things in my life started to happen, I became extremely depressed. Couldn't get out of bed and wasn't in the mood to talk to anyone. I did my best to still participate in daily life but was burning inside every day. I literally cried every day for four months straight at least once a day. There were days I didn't want to get out of bed and I prayed a lot to get up. Many people didn't know because I went about building my business and smiling, but I was hurting very much. God definitely helped me through that time with random messages from people that I never really talked to. Family was there, and I received blessings I can't even explain. Books were randomly sent to me by people who connected me to certain things. That is another reason why I know He is real and there for you.

Depression is the feeling of truth hitting you; a disappointment that owns you and your joy. It's really a choice to feel that way. As I have struggled with moments like that, I realize that it was because I was lacking the 7 Rocks of Life. I was imbalanced, and the reason why I share this book and choose to be vulnerable and open is that I know many people battle with these same things. But if you're going through this, second guessing things about life or yourself, or just want true freedom and to get yourself out of this mental prison, I want you to know you can get through this!

"NEVER MAKE YOUR LOWS IN LIFE KEEP YOU DOWN; MAKE THEM YOUR REASON WHY YOU GOT BACK UP."

Sometimes your mistakes are Gods way of teaching you. In your spiritual walk, you will learn the principles of life you should follow. You will gain wisdom and clarity of the understanding of life and the power of forgiveness.

Here is something interesting my sister messaged me recently that my niece had said:

Niece: This is my homework.

Sister: You get homework from school?

Niece: No, this is my home, and that is my work (pointing to a letter-tracing book on her kid table). This place is my "home-work."

When I received this text, I said wow! This life we live in is our "home" and the things we learn or do is our "work." But to understand our work in this life, we need to read the proper manual to get the "home-work" done. Your life and your mission are the homework we all need to do every day. When you seek the proper homework that you should be doing, you will gain peace, and you will not react to everything. You will learn how to respond to things in God's way. You will develop a vibe around you that will attract a great tribe around you. Those who can't be alone find it is because they live in other people's homes and forget to take care of their own home and work. Create a heaven on earth in your life so that your home-work of life will be seen by others. You will see that your walk of life will become your story that others feel and see.

"Stories that inspire with people that you will admire."

—SeVen RoCk LiFe Podcast

Be Unlike Your Enemy

I remember hearing a story about a man who saw a snake being burned, and he decided to take it out of the fire. When he did that, the snake bit him badly.

He dropped the snake, and it fell right back into the fire. The man grabbed a metal pole and took the snake out of the fire to save his life.

Someone who had been watching approached the man and said, "That snake bit you. Why are you still trying to save it?"

The man replied, "It is the nature of the snake to bite, but that's not going to change my nature, which is to help."

Do not change your nature simply because someone harms you. Do not lose your good heart, instead learn to take precautions.

Too often, we let other actions be the thing that changes our heart or spirit. Learn to be unlike those who hurt you because if you are the same, you are just as guilty as they are.

"GOD DOESN'T LIKE GOSSIP; HE WANTS PEACE."

There was another story I read about a man whose son was shot. The father of a pizza delivery driver was able to somehow find empathy and forgive the boy who played a role in the murder of his son. He was sentenced to 31 years in prison. Two years before this, his wife had passed away as well. In his faith, he believes God will not forgive someone until the person who was wronged forgives the person who wrongs him. He said to the young boy, "I am angry at the devil for misguiding you and misleading you to do such a horrible crime, but I forgive you."

Sometimes, not forgiving imprisons us from our joy and peace of life. This is a hard place to get to. The situation this dad dealt with would be difficult for me or anyone, but he had a strong faith which freed himself from bitterness and a life of hate. This story inspired me not to let the little things of life carry on. It's extra weight that is not needed. Don't always try to be victorious over others; learn to create peace.

"THE FIRST TO APOLOGIZE IS THE BRAVEST, THE FIRST TO FORGIVE IS THE STRONGEST, AND THE FIRST TO FORGET IS THE HAPPIEST."

BUILDING YOUR HOME FIRST

Some of you enjoy going to friends' or family's home a lot because it's probably a great environment with great food or drinks. Their fridge is always fully stocked right, and you are living on a budget. You have the "if it's free, it's for me" mentality. But you forgot to build your own home. You were too busy living in someone else's instead of building yours. You see this especially in the world of social media. You live in other people's lives, and then years go by, and you realize that you never built a home and have nowhere to live. That's why no one ever asked if they could come over. You never built a home that attracts people.

That's why leadership is truly all about positive influence. We will speak more about that later, but it's important in building your home. That's why you often see relationships with two empty people not lasting long. This is also true if one person is full, but the other is empty. It's an internal problem they must solve on their own. For me, it was my walk in my spiritual life. I felt I needed someone in my life to be fulfilled. Yes, it's nice to find that soulmate or person with whom to share your life, but you must have a full home because your spouse or friend do not determine your happiness. Yes, some people are important, but it's a dangerous spot to be in because you must build two separate homes that eventually connect to make a mansion or a town or city that has beauty together. I've been in relationships where one of us forgot who the other was. You must have an individuality that combines to make something special. We will talk about relationships more in that rock of life.

Your spiritual walk will be something that will turn you from a cup into a pitcher that will pour into people's lives. Always remember that the trials and challenges you are currently going through are a test for your testimony that one day you'll be able to share. I remember this past Christmas Eve. Being alone during the holidays, I felt like the world was against me and there was no one to support me. I had a burning sensation in my heart and couldn't stop crying that day.

I remember going to my parents' house and trying to get myself together emotionally. For some reason, that day was really tough, and I'll never forget what happened next. I went into my backyard where I grew up playing baseball and learning the game. I had spent a lot of time there, and my life was flashing by with all of my childhood memories. My sister came outside to support me because she had been through similar emotions in her life. She was the only one at that time who understood how I was feeling. I went back inside and sat on the couch at my parents' home (someone else's home) and stared outside, crying, and watching my niece playing. I felt paralyzed somehow.

I ended up having to leave and going back home because I felt bad about my attitude and wanted my family to enjoy Christmas Eve. I was driving down the dark roads and thinking about my life. In fact, I questioned if life was even worth living that night. Should I drive straight or go into the woods? That's how deep and down I was at that point of my life. By God's grace he kept me going straight on that road that evening. My relationship was gone, certain friends were not there, and I had no one with whom I felt I could turn to or enjoy the holidays with. Last year at the same time, I had all my family over enjoying Christmas Eve, and twelve months later, I was by myself. By the grace of God, I stayed straight that night. I went back home and realized my church was having a Christmas Eve mass, so I went by myself. I sat to the left in the corner and just waited for it to start.

That day was my most broken day but also my most liberating day. Before mass started, there was a gentleman there (now a great friend) who had sat down with me a few times during my struggles the past few months. He didn't know me, but he knew I was broken. I guess God told him and he opened his arms to be there for me.

Recently, we were talking, and I was sharing with him about this book and other things happening in my life. He said he remembered that night, as well.

That Christmas Eve, he walked by me and gave me a handshake and a quick hug because he was in a rush. Then, out of nowhere, he came back less than a minute later to give me a big hug, and said, "I love you, and God loves you. You are going to do big things for this world!"

"SOMETIMES A HUG AND AN 'I LOVE YOU' CAN SAVE SOMEONE'S LIFE."

He didn't know how dark that night was for me and that an hour before that I was ready to end my life. He said that when he said hello quickly and kept walking that he felt as if a wall went up in front of him and that God made him turn around to come back. I got chills when he told me that, and I told him it was one of the things that saved my life. That meant everything to me, and he is a great man doing amazing things in the communities.

The pastor that night was his dad who started speaking about the birth of Jesus and His life. He talked about knowing that He gave us life every day for his sacrifices and we would need to have rebirth at times in our life. Once I heard that, something hit my soul and heart strongly. I decided to have a rebirth in my life, and my journey started to shift from being depressed to being very optimistic about the future. I left that church renewed and with a peace that I can't describe.

"YOU WILL NOT WIN YOUR WARS IN LIFE BY
RUNNING AWAY FROM YOUR BATTLES."

Ever since that evening, my whole life started to shift little by little. Four months of pain and confusion started to move forward in a positive direction. I went to a friend's house who recently got married at my house that summer as I was going through everything. That night on Christmas Eve, they welcomed me over for some great company after church. They really are a beautiful couple inside and out, and it meant a lot to me. We had a great time, and seeing the kids open presents put a smile on my face and made me realize how renewing kids can be with their joy and happiness. Plus, having this cute little pitbull dog on my lap helped out, too. I went home, looked up at the ceiling, and said to God, "Please help me become a better person, someone who's home is truly filled inside. I forgot to truly build my home with You inside of it leading the way."

Twenty minutes later, I messaged my family and said I would be a new man tomorrow and we would celebrate Christmas in NYC and go see the tree! It was an amazing time. We will never forget that day, my family says. The moral of the story is that when you feel you're alone, He's always there. You need to submit and put your heart out there for Him, and He will truly redesign your home to make it better, stronger, and the way He wanted you to be in the first place.

Sometimes the only way your brokenness gets fixed is something only you and God can take care of together. Having a great counselor can help you understand the world and be there for you to discover what needs to change. That comes from having an honest conversation with them. My counselor helped me so much during this time, and I am grateful for that person in my life. Learn to put God first and watch the type of house and identity He builds for you. There is always a greater purpose to the pain you're going through. Find something bigger than you, and giving up will never cross your mind.

"YOUR IMAGE OF YOURSELF WILL DETERMINE THE DEPTH OF INTIMACY YOU WILL HAVE WITH GOD."

Just remember, you may not always be in control of what happens around you, but you are in control of what happens in you. Sometimes, we have this "inner me" and "enemy" that tries to control us. Don't let the enemy defeat your inner me. Have the right sources in life guiding you through that journey. Faith makes things possible, not necessarily easy.

My brother asked me a question once while we were driving to Vermont to go skiing. He asked, "On that day, Dec 24th, while you were driving on the highway, what made you not give up on your life at that moment?"

When he asked that, many things flashed in front of me thinking of what kept me going home then to the church that night. I said to him, "Honestly, bro, it was three things. One, I would be letting God down if I just gave up on this great life we have been given. We are all here on such a thin thread it's crazy! Two, my family and you all, I would truly be letting you down. I know you guys counted on me to be that light and dreamer of the family, to be that spark to light up each other's lives, and three, every day I would get phone calls and texts from people I was mentoring, and they counted on me being that rock in their lives." I felt at times I was a very soft and fragile rock, but they meant way too much just to give up. They were family to me, and I owed it to them to make it through this season. I started to tear up, and we got all emotional in the car, and my brother said something to me that touched my heart. I am very grateful to have my brother back. He said, "I love you and will always be there for you. I wouldn't have anyone to go skiing with, but now we get to hit the slopes together and enjoy this gift of life!" That meant the world to me, and when I felt the world gave up on me, I had my brother and family there, those I am blessed to mentor, and of course, the man above—God!

"WHEN PEOPLE SAY THEY ARE SELF-MADE,
I ALWAYS SAY TO REMEMBER YOU ARE
FIRST GOD-MADE."

SEEDS PLANTED

You will not reap *where* you sow; you will reap *what* you sow. I think nature and gardens produce some of the best life lessons we can learn. Think about this:

The seed is you

The soil is the environment
The water is life and hope
The fertilizer is wisdom
The sun is God/Heart

There are seasons when you will produce a great harvest, but there are also seasons where you will struggle due to storms. Be sure to prepare for those seasons with the right faith or food to store to survive. The biggest thing that has helped me through my season of struggle has been faith and the Man above. We can't always rely on our neighbors because they also have a family to feed.

We sometimes plant these seeds in life, and they don't produce fruit as quickly as you want. You might check the seed every day and move the dirt, which you don't realize is ruining its root system and growth. I have often tried to rush things, but the reality is that certain things just take time. You need to be patient because sometimes it's growing under the soil so that when it sees daylight, its root system is strong, and it springs up. Bamboo is a fast-growing tree that can grow up to 35 inches per day. It can grow 80 feet tall in 6 weeks. But did you know that in the first 4 years, it does not even break the soil? That is because, for it to grow that tall, its root system must be strong. Harvest may not happen in life when you are not focused on the soil and root system.

SPIRITUAL

"SOMETIMES WE WANT THE TREE, THE RESULT,
BUT WE FORGET WE NEED TO SECURE THE
ROOTS FIRST."

We may die in the flesh, but we never die in spirit. The seeds we plant in our family, friends, and the world eventually give a harvest. I had a great friend who I respected very much pass away last year. He and his wife were truly such heartfelt and great people to be around unfortunately he passed unexpectedly, but he taught me a lot in the time I was around him. Although I was his mentor, I learned from him. I realized:

"YOU CAN'T LEARN EVERYTHING FROM SOMEONE,
BUT YOU CAN LEARN SOMETHING FROM
EVERYONE."

Kermitt was a Vietnam War Veteran who was an officer and fighter pilot who flew F-111s. He dealt with many flashbacks from that time that affected him and also dealt with upbringing issues. His life was a battle, and he was constantly fighting but always trying to overcome because he was a winner. I saw him in his later years battle with keeping his six-figure jobs and supporting his family. He was very good at being an IT professional, but jobs would come and go in that world. It was tough at times for the family, but they always fought and never gave up.

The one thing I took away most from Kermitt was his smile, energy, and positive outlook on life. He was a grateful man who was fighting a battle inside his whole life. The truth is that we all are fighting in our own ways. I would see him show up for Bible study, growing to be a better man for his family, kids, and society. He planted a seed in me and many others by having love, being a fighter, and always smiling. Man, his smile was good, and his laugh was heard from miles away. His music was truly amazing as well. He loved the sounds and could play piano just like Billy Joel (I think better). He was creative and was a talented musician. As I am writing this right now, I am smiling because he truly never died. His flesh may be gone, but his spirit carries on through his amazing, strong wife whom I consider a great friend, his kids, myself, and now, through this book, to the world.

Remember that one day we will not be here in the flesh, but our spirit will be carried on. What will you plant for others to learn or feel so that your legacy continues to carry on because you lived?

Thank you to all who have served this country in all different ways. God bless you and your family for your selfless sacrifice. Your service is greatly appreciated.

GIFT OF LIFE

Many times, we look up and down and at others. We look all over the place for the gift of life. We seek so much, but sometimes people go throughout their whole life never finding it. Do me a favor and find a mirror or reflection. Look really hard into it. What do you see? A reflection of you? You are the gift of life.

Each one of us in this world has been uniquely made with different fingerprints, looks, and so much more. The best gift this world has been given is you, and then everything else follows behind that: family, kids, job, business friends, etc. We forget that our gift is life, and what we do with that life is up to us. Our story of how we got here in this moment is what makes us so individually unique. I'm not sure what your story will be. You and God are the designers of that. I think sometimes we don't know the hidden gifts we have, whether it is helping people, being able to public speak, being a great mother or father, performer, or even being able to write.

Growing up, I wrote poems all the time; they just flowed for me. Fast forward 31 years later, and I'm writing my first book to inspire and help people live better lives and raise money to give back to deprived communities. With what I've learned and continue to learn along this journey, I know we must find out what we have been gifted with. Realize that *you* are the gift of life, what will you give and to whom will you give it?

THE RIGHT SOURCES IN LIFE

Approval is something we chase as a kid, but as we get older, seeking approval from the wrong sources in life will make us tired, let us down, and make us feel empty. We look for validation from friends, strangers, and even social media. If those things don't validate us, we go crazy and get upset or even depressed. We have all been there thinking that the world doesn't like us. I've realized that:

"IT'S NOT YOUR TASK TO BE LIKED. YOUR TASK IS
TO BE LIKABLE, AND IT IS SOMEONE ELSE'S TASK
TO EITHER LIKE YOU OR NOT."

How simple is that! We try to get everyone to approve of us, but then we don't approve of ourselves. When I started doing that and approving my relationship with God, life became so much more simple. Think of a time when a friend got mad at you because you didn't call them, or something happened that was truly silly, and they stopped talking to you. They ignore you and are bitter. Stop trying to make that your problem. It's their problem, so go on with your life. Do what you can but know that it's not your job to get them to be happy about you again. Say you're sorry, but that's about it. Take a real audit to see if you did something that needs to be fixed, but if you didn't, you're good! I used to let this sit in me and ask what was wrong with me. Of course, we can change, but relationships, which I go over later, are like seasons. They change every few months or years.

Our friendships change, but you need to make sure you have the right source in your life. Also, when you look for approval and information from everyone instead of your heart, especially in relationships, you go crazy. Trust me, you get answers in life but only when you're seeking the right knowledge from the right places and sources. My source has been studying the Bible. The knowledge and stories in the Bible have truly changed my perspective of situations. I used to get upset at things that I couldn't control.

I've learned to give up control at those times when I knew I couldn't change anything. I remember getting shingles at 25 years old because of stress. I would always let things bother me so much. Whether it was money, friends, relationships, or business, I would get heated, but nothing changed. That's because I wasn't plugged into the right source. When you charge an electric car, do you use the same plug as you do for a toaster? It's different because you need a bigger source of power to charge that car properly.

Friends, mentors, and other people can help you, but there comes the point where they can no longer help you, and you need to go with you and God. Understanding this changed my life. It brought true peace and understanding. God's texting you, but you're spending too much time on your email or social media, and you're not checking your spiritual inbox where he's trying to get your attention.

"I THANK GOD FOR BEING THERE DURING MY LONELIEST TIME IN LIFE, FOR BEING MY SOURCE TO PUSH ME THROUGH THE ADVERSITY AND TRIALS. LEAN ON HIM, AND YOU WILL GET UNDERSTANDING."

CHAINS OF LIFE

Some of you may have abandonment issues. Maybe you were adopted, or your parents divorced or did drugs, and now you feel resentment toward them. I understand that anger or hurt inside comes out sometimes. But I think our perspective has to shift.

Look at the blessings that come from being alive in this beautiful world.

I remember speaking to someone whose father left them and got remarried. This person had anger building up inside of them. I told them I could understand their pain, but they were in a prison they created because of someone else's actions. Let's say your dad did something bad and got locked up, and you decided to get locked up with them. Ten years go by, and you get out of prison. When your friends and family see you after ten years, they ask what happened to you. You say you locked yourself up with your dad because of what he did. You did nothing, but you chose to let his actions affect your life. It caused you to go into a mental and real prison when you could have been enjoying the past ten years in freedom. You also hurt everyone around you because you took yourself away from those who cared about you. Be thankful for what your parents have or haven't done.

They also have their own story of why they are who they are. Learn to break that generational curse or chain of life to become better for the next people in your family or life. Sometimes, you are the only example your kids or strangers will see. Learn to let your feet be louder than your tongue in the blueprint of life.

Pastor Steven Furtick of Elevation Church said:

CHAIN stands for:

Choice

Habit
Automatic
Identity
Nature

These patterns of life become our choice if we take them with us; they become a habit we do every day that people see and feel, which becomes an automatic thing to us without trying. It's what we are known for, which is our identity and that's why people will be like, "Oh, Mary is always that way; its who she is," and it becomes part of your nature. Learn to break those chains and start a new pattern in your life. We sometimes know another person's identity better then we know ours. Learn to make your true identity the nature of who you are.

"YOUR CIRCUMSTANCES OF LIFE DON'T DEFINE YOU; YOUR IDENTITY OF WHO YOU TRULY ARE DOES."

ROOT SYSTEM

If a tree's roots are not deep enough, a strong wind or storm can knock it down and uproot it. When your roots of life, standards, and moral compass are strong, you will not be uprooted by society's pressure. Culture sometimes forces us to be someone other than who we want to be. It's like peer pressure, but I call it culture pressure. Knowing how you should treat people, fight for your relationships, put people over profits, etc. is key to being truly rooted.

Sometimes, we need to create that new story and knock down that old tree to let a new one grow. It hurts, and it's work, but you will have a stronger tree that will survive those storms. I look at people who battle sickness such as cancer, and I commend them so much because, through those trials and storms, they get knocked down but remain faithful and have so much fruit and blessings that arise from that struggle. Our roots are attacked by termites every day, but you need to work on your spiritual rock to make sure they don't get to the roots and the inside of your trunk or body of life. Trees can look good from the outside, but it's the roots and trunk that holds it up.

Father and Mother Power

I put this after the root system because I never realized how strong a parent's upbringing affected your root system until recently. I'm sure many of you can relate to this, but sometimes our parents do things we wonder about, or sometimes they don't show the love we want. I think it comes down to taking the time to hear your parent's story. We know where our parents live, but we don't know where they came from and how they truly grew up. We don't know the story of their childhood, whether they grew up with parents who may have hurt them and changed their root system, which tremendously affects who they are.

Before I launched this book, I shared at breakfast with my parents the part that I just spoke about above about the kid and dad in prison together. As I was reading that, my father teared up, which I had never seen him do. At that moment, I realized his relationship with his father was broken, which really put clarity in my life to understand some of his actions. At times, I said he did not know how to express affection because he was always tough as I got older. He tended to give a handshake hello and fist pump instead of a hug.

Things have changed a little, but I found out he grew up with no affection and love from his father. This affected him a lot even though his mother gave him a lot of love. There was a lot of hurt, and at times, he felt kicked to the road with no support. You have an earthly father and a heavenly father, and unfortunately, our earthly fathers are not perfect. Sometimes, our parents build a fortress around their hearts to protect their pain from growing up. But you need to love them no matter what because that's the very thing that will soften their hearts over time. I think we often try to prove our parents wrong, but God wants us to honor them instead and love them no matter what.

I remember the day I received a text that rocked my world. *Your father had a heart attack and is in the hospital in the emergency room.* My heart sank into my stomach. I finished my meeting and drove as quickly as possible to Stony Brook University, which is a phenomenal hospital. On the way, I got pulled over because of how fast I was going, but the police officer let me go because of my situation. I got to the hospital, and I broke down when I saw my dad. Thankfully, he was okay, and they had put stents in his heart, but seeing him so weak and hooked up to all of those tubes made me realize how special life really is. I cried a lot that evening, and I also prayed a lot. I thought about how everything precious to us can be gone in a second. That was a life-changing moment for me, and a wake-up call to cherish and honor my parents no matter what. Thankfully, my dad is fully recovered and by the grace of God, stronger than ever.

"IT'S NOT ALWAYS ABOUT BEING VICTORIOUS; IT'S ABOUT BEING PEACEFUL."

If you feel like your parents are a liability, maybe because of drugs or bad decisions they have made, love them from a distance. Do as much as you can, and pray for them, but don't carry anger because it will imprison you. I saw my mom's love for her father, and I also have many fond memories of him, but her mom would get angry and upset while my grandpa would not react but just be cool. But my grandma's upbringing was rough and probably affected her a certain way, and she never got better with those things and carried them through her life. What my grandma did teach my mom, however, was to be able to live with simple things. The refrigerator could be empty, and Grandma would create some type of meal, and she passed that on to my mom. I know many of you do that where you look in the fridge five times to see if there is anything in there. Nothing changes every time you look but we are praying for something to show up. Am I right? But the thing that was left from what her mom taught her was that while we see nothing in the fridge, she sees something to make. Our flesh may pass, but our spirit continues to live on with those we impacted and lessons we were taught along our journey of life. Our parents brought us into this world, so be grateful for even their imperfections because there are root systems they come from. Instead of expecting so much, why not ask what can you do as a son or daughter to make their life easier. If you remember that everyone in this world is God's child, you'll want to respect and honor your parents. Take what you learn that is good and break those chains of things that are bad. Learn to honor your family with the life you live and the legacy you carry on.

"PARENTS ARE LIKE ROCKS. SOME ARE SMOOTH, AND SOME ARE ROUGH, BUT AT THE END OF THE DAY, IF YOU NEED A PLACE TO SIT, YOU CAN COUNT ON THEM TO BE THERE."

FAITH

Faith is the complete trust or confidence in someone or something. It's about believing it will happen. You don't know *how* it will happen, but you know it will. Sometimes, our life doesn't turn out the way we thought it would. You go down a road that is unfamiliar and must continue driving until you find the road you were supposed to be on. Throughout my life, there have been times when I said the road didn't look familiar. For example, I remember being crushed when my baseball career was over.

I had my business, but I thought baseball was my future until I hit a wall and hung up my shoes. I remember going into that locker room and getting my name called that I was cut for the season. My heart sank, and I went straight to a golf range to hit. I then sat on a hill overlooking Grand Traverse Bay in Michigan, just staring for two hours. I liked baseball, but I loved helping people and inspiring them. Fast forward seven years, and I'm writing this book to give back to others what I've learned during this journey of life.

Trusting is sometimes a hard thing to do, but faith is like being on a boat. You trust the boat will float and that the captain is good at his job. You realize you don't have control, so you relax and let the captain do the work. Let God be your captain. You did your job to get on the boat, but it's not your job to steer it. God will give you a tree in life, but it's your job to make a table from that tree. You need to have faith that one day someone will use or buy that table from you, but you will never know unless you first make that table from the tree, He gave you.

"YOUR TRANSPARENCY AND FAITH IN LIFE WILL LEAD TO TRANSFORMATION."

STRONG COMMUNITIES

Have you ever seen a sign for a town that says something like: Great Place to Raise a Family? That shows a strong community and environment that is safe for raising kids and a family. You may not have been blessed to be in one of those communities, but you can ensure the community is strong within your home, with the people you are around, and the places where you spend time.

Faith-based and principal-based communities are key to keeping you on track. When you think about a strong community, a negative person can be put into one and will change very quickly because of the surroundings and environment. Think about a dying plant that is put outside in the sun with warm air and it starts to come alive again. Even a cold piece of coal if put back in the fire will become hot and alive again.

Communities are also a place that gives love and forgiveness when you need it. But be careful not to rely on this one thing as a source because it won't always be there, and people will grow tired of you talking about the same old story. That's why you need approval from the Main Source. But spending time in supportive communities is key, which is why Bible studies or churches are key to keeping you on track with that. Always remember that church or where you fellowship is not just a place but people who work on becoming better every day following Godly principles.

"GOD'S FAVORITE ECONOMY IS ABOUT GIVING, SO MAKE SURE YOU'RE IN ALIGNMENT WITH HIS BELIEFS."

ONLINE VS. OFFLINE IMAGE

In today's society, we work so hard to build this brand and online image that we forget to build our offline image. The offline image is the real you that lives in the real world, not just the online world. I've seen people post pictures of this "phantom" lifestyle and they are still living at home with their parents. Online images are today's business card, so it's important but make sure it matches who you truly are. Many people plan more for a vacation than they do for their life, faith, or work.

God made you in a unique way, but you must discover your hidden talents and become who you were truly destined to be. If your offline image is not strong, there will be times in your life that will break you and expose you. This has happened in my life, and honestly, it's been one of the best things that have happened to me. I remember hearing an interview with A-Rod (played baseball with the NY Yankees and was an All-Star player) about how he got caught taking steroids and had to sit out for a year and how that crushed him! Now, then years later, he said that year changed him and taught him so much about himself. Learn to strip yourself of all the identities society or the world has given you. If you rely on only those identities, you will eventually lose who you are and take away your true peace.

"BEING ALONE IS SOMETIMES THE FIRST TIME YOU TRULY GET TO KNOW YOURSELF."

These breakdowns in life help us if we learn from them and change. Work on your offline image more. Stop trying to chase other people's images and chase the one that God wants you to have that you can truly feel good about. If a home looks really good on the outside, people will come to look at it. But if there are no furniture, food, or games inside to enjoy, people will leave unimpressed. Do not build your identity and value systems only on image, position, power, or performance. Remember, your worth has nothing to do with your social media following.

GOD'S PLAN

In wrapping up this chapter, your spiritual walk in life is the first rock you need to put in your cup. It's your foundation in life. You can try to do it quickly, but with any home, when you rush the foundation, you will eventually see cracks. If you want your home, your offline image, to be real and authentic, make this the most important journey you embark on. The biggest things that helped me get through this time that will also help you was communities of great people, certain audios or podcasts of people to whom I related, and finding someone who had strong roots in this part of life to share. What you're learning will also develop in your alone time of praying or meditating and will help you gain an understanding of yourself and the things you're learning.

> "IF GOD REFINED YOU, DESIGNED YOU AND
> CREATED YOU, WHY ARE YOU LETTING THE
> WRONG PEOPLE TRY TO EDIT YOU!"

Always remember, it only takes one coal that's hot to heat up the others around it. Even when a lot of coals are cold, one that is still warm can spark the others around. Community and environment are a huge support system, but if everyone around you is like those coals that are cold, nothing will catch on fire. You must catch the hot flame of God from the inside on your spiritual walk. It will start inside you with your spirit and heart.

That Christmas Day, I decided to start a rebirth of my life knowing it wouldn't be easy and I would continue to fail, but as long as I truly have Him, I'm not worried about anything else. What's interesting is that at that time I was not writing a book or doing any projects at all. I was too broken and not in a position to. Fast forward two weeks later, and I started getting signs of things to start doing and creating by the Man above. Your test of life will one day be your testimony of life.

> "IN LIFE, BE VERY CAREFUL WHO YOU TALK TO
> ABOUT WHAT GOD MAY BE DOING INSIDE YOU.
> BE CAREFUL ABOUT WHO YOU COMMUNICATE
> WITH ABOUT THE IMPRESSIONS OF WHAT GOD
> IS STEERING INSIDE YOU. IF YOU SHARE THE
> RIGHT IDEA TO THE WRONG PEOPLE, YOUR IDEA
> WILL DIE BEFORE IT HAD THE OPPORTUNITY
> TO CONCEIVE AND GIVE BIRTH TO WHAT

GOD IS DOING IN YOUR LIFE."
—STEVEN FURTICK

By taking care of the flame of life inside of you, you will naturally start to help ignite others' flames around you, not by what you say, but how you start to live. Remember, one spark in the woods can ignite everything on fire. The flick inside of you will start to be shared all around you in a positive way. It is not about talking about what you're learning or doing, it's about showing it through your actions of love, patience, understanding, growing, and so much more.

"LEARN TO LET YOUR FEET BE LOUDER THAN YOUR TONGUE."

Sometimes, silence is the best way to discover you and your relationship with your higher power. That silence will be heard from others by the actions you take going forward and the harvest that starts to happen from what you're applying in life because you have a great tour guide called God helping you. Always realize you are enough and that God took twelve average people to lead the world to speak about the lessons that were taught. Never think you are not enough; it comes in God's time when you are truly available. You need to read the manual of life to understand how we are supposed to operate on this journey. With God on your side, you can't lose. He is the best teammate and coach you can have. It's like having Tom Brady on your pickup football game with your friends. God is the best quarterback throwing and calling the plays for your life, but you need to make sure you're listening so that you are in the right spot to score the most important touchdown, which is this beautiful life we have been given.

"GOD WANTS OUR HEARTS, NOT OUR STUFF. HE HAS A POEM HE WROTE FOR EACH ONE OF US, SO MAKE SURE YOU ARE READING THE RIGHT POEM."

QUIZ

Rate this Rock for yourself on a scale from 1–10.

_____

_____

What was your top take-away from this chapter?

_____

_____

What gaps do you have in this Rock?

_____

_____

What is your game plan and action to fix these gaps?

_____

_____

2

RELATIONSHIPS

If you were a seed that would turn into a big tree, and you were planted in concrete, would you ever grow? Nope, wrong environment. Would you expect a palm tree to grow up north in cold weather? This is a false expectation due to the wrong environment. That's why I believe your circle of friends and the environment you place yourself in is so vital to your success in this game of life. I like to call it relational life support. It's the support you need to build a life with great relationships. You are similar to a garden.

- The soil is your environment

- The water is your wisdom

- The sun are the people that shine in your life

- The seeds are you and your circle of people

Put all of those together and BOOM! A tree with fruit starts to grow. You become a pitcher not just a cup to pour into others. A cup you can only drink from, but a pitcher you can pour into others' lives and still have some left for you.

But you will realize in life that some people are a tree but only have branches and twigs, no leaves or fruit in life to give out. That's okay. People are either an asset or a liability in your life. If you think about the word "diet," it means to restrict oneself to small amounts or specific kinds of food to lose weight.

In life, you may need to diet and restrict yourself with the people around you. It's called pruning or "life dieting." Sometimes, people put things upon you that are fatty, weigh you down, and make you sick. Learn to cut those people out of your diet so that you get healthier and live a better life.

Learn to be around good people and new people and avoid those who tell the same old story. Strangers are waiting for you to become friends with them. You want to be around friends who make you want to perform and level up to those high standards, to be a better person, clean the house before they come over, dress nicer, and be cleaner in all areas of your life.

At times, I was a liability to society and had to work on being a better man, person, and friend. I still have to work on that today. You will go through seasons like that, and that's called pruning so that eventually it grows back stronger and better. My spiritual/leadership counselor said to me one time that to go higher in life, you sometimes have to go deeper to build a higher building. How true is that! It hurts. It sucks. You cry. You are depressed, but if you are available and patient, you will be happy with what is created. It's easy to stay comfortable in life, but if you push through, there are rewards at the next level, especially with meeting new people.

As a great example, I have a hot tub about 60 feet away from the house. Winter is the best time to use it, especially when it's 20 degrees outside. But when people who have never experienced that before look at me and say I'm crazy. I have to convince them to trust me walking or running the 60 feet to the hot tub. It's scary and cold, but when you get into that tub, and it's 102 degrees—man! You feel amazing with nature, and the warm water and jets hit your back in all of the right places. You sit there for about 45 minutes, talking and enjoying the experience, and then you realize you are pruning like a grape and need to get out. Fear kicks in again at the thought of getting out of the hot tub into the cold weather, but what they don't know is that your body is so hot you have about 45 seconds to dry and get back inside the house, and you won't feel the cold. At first, this experience was scary, but eventually it opened up a new perspective you want to repeat. It is the same thing with a relationship. After all is said and done, you're like, wow, that was really nice getting to know that person, and I would love to meet them again and hang out.

Choosing your surroundings is key to many areas of your life, such as standards, values, and even income. If you add up the incomes of the five people you hang out with the most, and most likely, yours will be the average of those five.

Let's take this to the next level. There are two types of people in life: those who are surviving and those who are thriving to be better. There is nothing wrong with either one, but one is existing, and one is truly living to be better.

You will notice that certain friends and family in your life are going about their day and their life merely getting by, and that's about it. They live the same mundane life, day after day. This doesn't make them bad people, but sometimes they become the weight in your vehicle that you're driving toward your destination. If you don't let some of them out, it will hold you back from whatever you are trying to accomplish and burn more gas in your vehicle of life.

You'll notice these people talk about entertainment, sports, or the good old days. These are not bad things to talk about sometimes, but not all the time. Thrivers talk about new podcasts, new books, dreams, ideas, family, and the future. Survivors gossip a lot, and thrivers speak about moving forward and not living the same old story. Thrivers find solutions; survivors find excuses. The list goes on and on, so take an audit to see who in your life is pouring into you while you are pouring into them. See who is moving forward, not just living in the rearview mirror.

WESTERN VS. EASTERN CULTURE

When you look at "primitive" tribes, you'll find that the community is key to their survival. In Eastern cultures, there is more of a "help me, help you" mentality, that's how we can work together to prosper and grow. That's why you'll see certain cultures come here to America and do well quickly because they understand the law of unity. They might work together to buy a building with the extended family living there and paying it off quickly so they can use it as income and buy another one. Sometimes, owners of restaurants will have their kids work at the restaurant because it's part of the family income to survive, or they will have to take their income the business brings in and turn it into salaries for others to work there. Also, they will support each other's business more so that they keep the money in the family. There is no right or wrong way to live, but this mentality can help build a strong community and even nation. They work to complete each other not compete against each other.

Here are some key differences between the East and the West:

Eastern (Asia and the Middle East)

- More conservative

- Taboo topics and very closed, tend to hide feelings

- Hindu, Buddhism, Islam, Jainism, Shenism, Taoism

- Elders are leaders of their family

- Children take care of their aging parents

- Complete each other by working together

- Arranged marriages, love comes after marriage

- More rigid with education

- Receivers of information

Western (North and South America and Europe)

- More open with feelings
- Jewish, Christian, and Islam
- Love comes before marriage
- Everyone decides their own future
- Competing against one another
- Creativity
- Older parents go into nursing homes
- Education promotes critical thinking and free thinking
- Information given is more interactive

If you look at the differences, it's very eye opening how each side goes about their life. The key factors are how their feelings are expressed, how they receive information and education, and how they compete with or complete each other. That last one is huge, and I think that if our world and especially our government understood the power of unity that it would be a better place and peace would exist.

STRANGERS BECOME FRIENDS

I was driving a while ago, and as I was driving, I looked at the windshield and then the rearview mirror and realized there was a reason why the rearview mirror was so much smaller than the windshield. The DMV and insurance companies don't want you looking so much behind you; they want you to look forward so that you're safer and can see what's coming up in front of you.

You can't drive using the rearview mirror all of the time. This is also true with people who live in the past and those who create a future. Often, we make the people we grew up with the closest people in our life. It's like someone who went to the majors (in baseball) and then went back to play with those in the minors or even high school. Your craft and talent start to revert back to that level. That's not to say you can't spend time with those people because most likely they were there for you through your toughest times. Limit it and make sure their influence doesn't restrict you from your goals or dreams.

Some strangers you haven't met yet will be the people who add the most to your life. Embrace conversations with new people in life at places such as planes, coffee shops, restaurants, or the gym. The main reason why we are sometimes afraid to develop new friendships is that we feel we are not worthy or struggle with self-confidence. Realize something that the only difference between you and, say, a lawyer is that he or she studies their craft and has confidence. Learn more. Discover things that allow you to have conversations with all different types of people. Learn the art of asking questions. That is how you get to know someone. Ask questions like where are you from, how did you get into that career, where did you get those shoes, did you play sports, what have been your biggest life lessons up to this point, and so on.

> "WE ASK QUESTIONS AS KIDS GROWING UP
> TO LEARN, BUT FORGET TO DO THE SAME AS
> WE GET OLDER."

These simple questions open the door to unlimited conversations and potential great relationships, connections, and friends who add value to your life and open doors. If you never leave your ZIP code, you'll never discover how other people live.

I think back to meeting a young woman who sat next to me on the plane. We spoke about fitness and what she does, and she ended up dating someone I knew through baseball and business. A few months later, I connected with him for a workout, built our relationship, and then did a podcast on the 7 Rocks of Life with him and his partner. We now have a great friendship forming. What if I had put my headphones on, fell asleep, and never said hello?

Doors are closed every day for people because they forget to knock to see if anyone is home. Learn to break the ice with people who can lead you to amazing opportunities. I think about how I got into business when I was 20, and it was because someone left a voicemail on my phone my sophomore year. If I had not returned their call, I wouldn't be where I'm in life. I wouldn't be blessed with a great business, friends, and family.

Open doors every day you go out. Even if you never do business with them, you can make a difference in their life, and maybe they will make a difference in your life. Don't try to build a life completely by yourself. Seek out those who are ahead of you because they are potentially your shortcut. They might reduce the learning curve that you need to get to the next level.

"ALWAYS REMEMBER THAT THE FIRST SOCIAL MEDIA WAS HAVING NORMAL CONVERSATIONS IN PERSON. BEING SOCIAL DOESN'T HAVE TO BE JUST ONLINE; YOU CAN STILL DO IT OFFLINE."

RELATION TYPES

There are four types of relationships:

- Family

- Friendship

- Casual

- Romantic

You need to understand and choose which category the people you meet will be in or are in.

FAMILY

Obviously, family is family, but many times, friends become family. FAMILY stands for Forget About Me, I Love You. It's when you're able to be a selfless person and truly giving, sometimes forgetting about your own needs for the betterment of those whom you love like family. It doesn't always have to benefit you. I have had issues in the past understanding this, so realize that you will not always benefit from everything, and that's okay. Learn to have unconditional love toward everyone, not just on certain terms. With relationships there is repro-gramming or other things that need to be done to be better in this area of life, especially your spiritual journey.

Unfortunately, we live in a very narcissistic world, especially with social media that encourages us to focus on ourselves. We can become so self-consumed in our online identity that it becomes our only iden-tity. With this book, yes, my name is on it, but from the bottom of my heart, I write this for you to hopefully gain some wisdom or insight. I consider myself to still be a work in progress every day!

Family doesn't have to be someone who is related by blood to you; a friend can be family. With a "true" family member, it's someone who is there for you regardless of your situation in life.

"VALUE THOSE WHO SEE GREATNESS IN A PERSON
NO MATTER WHAT IMPERFECTIONS THEY
MAY HAVE."

As you get older, friendships change a lot and we question what's wrong with ourselves. When you hold a $5 bill close to your eyes, you don't see what it really is worth because it's too close. I think family and friendships are that way. They have greatness inside of them, but they are so close to you that you don't always see that greatness.

RELATIONSHIPS

Those people end up pruning themselves from your life, or eventually, your actions/results in life show them you had it in you all along. Because we see celebrities or athletes from so far away, they can appear perfect. We're not close enough to see their imperfections. At times, family or friends may love you only for what they can get from you or for how you make them feel. There may come a point where you need to let them go, unfortunately. It is really your choice because you're on a new journey that is about thriving and moving forward. Great friends accept you for who are, not what they want you to be, and they will push you to grow in a positive way. It's not always about being right in life. Sometimes you just need to forgive or apologize and move on. Remember, you will always have evidence in what you believe. We can all be "attorneys" in the journey of life, so don't always try to win. Look for peace and for the case to be solved, especially with family. We go through life being in "Life Court" with certain people, and honestly, it's a waste of time. Growing up, we loved our friends who were a little nutty, so embrace your nutty family members. Look at it as comedy instead of becoming angry. Love them for who they are, not who you want them to be. They are alive and here, so be grateful for that.

"AT CERTAIN TIMES, YOU NEED TO CREATE A NEW
SCRIPT IN LIFE, AND CERTAIN PEOPLE WILL NOT
BE IN THAT SCRIPT AT CERTAIN POINTS
OF YOUR LIFE."

PARENTS

With parents and relationships, you must be patient. They may do crazy things at times, but you need to love them anyway. Spend intentional time with them, especially if they are around in life. Cherish those moments and even the silly things they say or do. What's funny about older people or even very young kids is that they can get away with just about anything. People say, "Oh, he's old, that's why he did that or said that." I wish, at times, I had that old or young person power.

Six years ago, when I almost lost my father to a heart attack, I got a second chance to enjoy life with him. I'll be honest, at times I did and said things that weren't nice because I had my own issues. Recently, I realized something that my father's upbringing has played a huge role in who he is today. I spoke about that in the last chapter. He's truly an amazing person, and so is my mother. I am very blessed to have them as parents.

Your relationship with your parents is important, and you should learn how it affects the root system of who you are. For example, if your dad didn't have a good relationship with his dad, he can either be the same or different for his family. There will be traits about his dad that will be brought through into your relationship with your dad. If your dad never received love from his dad, you should show your dad love and appreciation. If you do the opposite, it will only remind him of his childhood, indirectly, and conflict will arise. Almost losing my dad made me more patient and grateful for him. Cherish that time with your parents no matter what they do. That's why the universe's favorite "law" is: Love always wins.

I was in Vermont on a ski trip and had two wonderful hosts where we were staying. We started to talk about their beautiful farm with the snow all around the land they owned, and how nature teaches us so many things. But I asked him a question about what his parents taught him while he was growing up because he spoke so highly of them and was just such a genuine man. He and his wife were heartfelt people. I love finding out about people's upbringings and what made them who they are today. I was able to get to know them while I was there, but I asked some questions just before we left, and their answers really opened my eyes.

I found out that they had raised nine children in the home we were staying in. Since both of them had been lovingly raised by such great parents, they felt the need to foster kids to give them what they might not have experienced otherwise. People would ask them why they took care of all those kids that weren't theirs, and they would respond, "Because everyone needs a rock to lean on sometimes, someone they can count on to be there for them when they need it." My heart became full because the whole time we were there, they were so inviting and peaceful. I will never forget them because they led their lives with their hearts, not just their minds.

"THERE IS NO SUCH THING AS BEING A PERFECT PARENT. IT'S ALL ABOUT BEING A REAL ONE THAT DOES THEIR BEST TO LOVE."

I don't have kids yet, but I am excited to be a father someday. I think back to why I loved my parents so much, and I think it was mostly their love and their strength. I was a firecracker, apparently, and had a lot of energy as a kid. If you have ever seen those leashes that people put on their kids—those were invented because of kids like me!

I remember one time when I was old enough to start going out by myself and be around different people, my parents said "We trust that you will do the right thing. You may be around people who don't, but that doesn't mean you need to do those things. We want to give you freedom but don't let our family down with the decisions you make." I was afraid to do drugs or smoke (I never have in my life) because I was afraid to disappoint them.

The other reason I respected my parents was that my dad is Sicilian, so I know who he was connected to. Also, he had this Bald Eagle belt buckle that was huge. That thing made me afraid of messing up. Sometimes, we value our freedom more when we see it taken away, and for me as a kid, trust and respect was key. The freedom they gave and also the environment they created at home was responsible for making me who I am today. I can always count on them to be my rock. Maybe you didn't have that, but I'm sure you had a friend, uncle, grandma, or aunt you could go to when you needed help. Be thankful for those who took care of you and became a great rock to lean on.

Casual

We spoke about casual relationships and people you meet who may become great connections or pour into your life while you pour into theirs. That's why personal growth and consuming content to make you a better person is key to relationships. People ask me how a causal relationship becomes a friendship, and when I looked at the times that happened to me, I realized three things:

1. There was vulnerability and authenticity that built trust.

2. They felt better about who they were becoming when they were around you.

3. They had a lot of fun, and it was truly enjoyable.

There are people who I've only known months, but it feels like I've known them for years. Relationships take work. There are times when you will see someone only one time, and that may be the only time you can leave a mark on that person with your smile, compliment, or genuine spirit. Sometimes, people might be hurting or going through a rough patch, and your compliment or just saying hi and getting to know them will mean the world to them. It may even save their life if they are questioning why they are here. (Trust me; it has happened to me.) We get caught up sometimes with so many of our own issues, and we sit next to someone and never say hello. Learn to have deeper conversations with people and get to know their story. A story will tell you a lot about a person's journey and where they are in life. You may even learn something from their experiences.

POWER OF LOVE

I think that with friends, relationships, and marriages that we sometimes are like a cavity in our tooth—extremely sensitive. We can be so easily offended.

"LOVE IS THE MOST POWERFUL LANGUAGE IN THE WORLD."

It was Valentine's Day as I was writing this chapter, and it was in my heart to send a few flowers to some people. This thought came to mind about love and the universal language that we all know. We know it, but sometimes we don't live it. Our hearts get jaded and hurt from all those years of having bad things happen to us. But I have realized that love is not so easily offended. Often, people will say "I'm fine," but "fine" really means "Feelings Inside Never Expressed." I wanted to share this poem I wrote last year when I was extremely down and going through my relationship issues and life in general. I wrote it in eight minutes because it just flowed from my heart.

What Is Love

Love is something that you feel,
It's something that can heal,
With every season we go through in life
We grow together husband and wife
With God all things are possible
Bonded together on his word
Through any struggle we encounter
He will fly over us like a bird
He will soar to catch us in our toughest times
Until he sees his work that truly shines
Miracles are spoken with faith and belief
But sometimes we don't see them, but we feel
    them and it gives us relief
Forgiveness is what holds us from love
Sometimes we ask God from up above
To help us through our darkest times
Be patient and you will see out of nowhere his
    love will truly shine
Love is a hard thing to do
It exposes our heart and feelings
But we truly never knew
The pain it can create internally
But at the same time, love can create beauty
    that becomes externally
It can create a world that allows you to be free
To smile and love no matter what we see
Just know if we live Gods way
What others speak will have no say
Love is patient
Love is kind

It does not envy,
It does not boast,
It is not proud.
It does not dishonor others
It is not self-seeking,
It is not easily angered,
It keeps no record of wrongs.
Love does not delight in evil but rejoices with
the truth.
It always protects, always trusts, always hopes,
and always perseveres.
Love never fails. (1 Corinthians 13: 4–8)

Love is a promise
Love is a souvenir
Once given and never forgotten
Never let it disappear.

–Steven Mazzurco, September 2018

In the Bible in Corinthians, it says that love is patient, love is kind, and love is not so easily offended. I've been overly sensitive at times in my relationships, whether it was with a spouse, parents, friends, or even mentors. We sometimes can be offended by the dumbest things. The way he/ she texted me or didn't say hi or didn't call me on my birthday, and then we build this bitterness that affects our relationships with everyone. One book I wish I had read years ago was Cherish by Gary Thomas. It is a great book on marriage and gives insight into what that word really means and why it is so powerful.

I've been there, and I still work on that to this day. A lot of that comes from a self-issue problem, and for me, it was spiritual. We look for so much approval from so many people, but we forget to get approval from our self and our higher power.

"You can't expect perfection in everything and everyone, or you will lose your joy and peace all the time."

I see it in the social media world we live in. Do you care about your Myspace friends and how many likes and comments you received? Probably not, because everyone stopped using it years ago, just like every other platform will disappear eventually. We hold onto things that life or people have done to us, but they're no longer an issue. They're done and over with. Those things you hold onto are just weight in your backpack holding you back from running as fast as you want to your goals or even new relationships.

"Old stories and negative talk are like expired milk. If you drink it, it makes you sick."

We often let past relationships affect our new ones, whether it is trust or respect or just used to being hurt. But if you want peace in your life, you can't expect perfection from everything and everyone. Your peace and joy will not happen if you expect everything to be perfect. Every day, work to accept and be graceful to everyone. We all have our own story in life that we bring to the table.

Friendships can come and go, but true friends will always come back. Sometimes we go into hibernation in certain seasons of life and need our space. Be kind and patient throughout those times for others. In my backyard, I have chipmunks that go away for the winter. I realize it's their time to rest, so why bother them if they are sleeping and hibernating. They will come back when the season is right. Some people's only image is their social media image, and they forget to build their real-life image. I've been there many times, and it can suck and play with your emotions. Some people count on approval from those "likes" to feel self-worth.

"IT IS NOT YOUR TASK IN LIFE TO BE LIKED. YOUR TASK IS TO BE LIKEABLE, AND UP TO THE OTHER PERSON TO LIKE YOU OR NOT."

We all know that sometimes our parents can appear to be off their rocker with the things they say or do. But sometimes you have to take a step back and love them no matter what and be grateful they are alive. Be grateful they gave birth to you, and that your mom carried you for nine months. You owe them for changing your diapers. They took care of you as a baby, and as they get older, you will take care of them. The cycle of life always happens.

A great man or woman takes care of one to two generations above them and one to two generations below them. Sometimes you need to be selfish for a short period to be selfless. This can help you to give back and put yourself in a great position to take care of those you love. It's like being on a plane, and if the oxygen mask comes down, you must put yours on first so that you then can help others around you. That may involve working hard and staying focused on your business or career for a certain amount of time so that you can give back later.

LIFESTYLE

Relationships or marriages take hard work, but if done right, it is extremely rewarding. I was married for two years, and when our relationship started dissolving, it changed my life. I went on an extreme journey of discovery of self-learning, auditing, and being broken and depressed, but it was a journey that God said I needed to go on if I wanted to get to the next level of life. The main reason why I wrote this book, became an entrepreneur, and mentor people is for one reason: to impact others. Yes, the lifestyle is great, but style with no life is empty.

I've learned that becoming that Proverbs 31 man is tough. It's not about knowing it or reading it; it's about living it. In the book Wild at Heart by John Eldredge, I discovered that every man wants three things in life:

1. An adventure to live

2. A battle to fight

3. A beauty to rescue

In his book Captivating, John Eldredge says that what every woman wants is:

1. To be swept up into a romance

2. To play an irreplaceable role in a great adventure

3. To be the beauty of the story

How true this is! In my opinion, marriages are failing because we are trying to do it culture's way instead of God's way. We sometimes don't identify and address the roots of our upbringing that we carry into our relationship and then wonder why it doesn't work.

Take me, for example. I had two years of what I thought was a good marriage, and then—Bam! —the bomb is dropped. One day I was speaking in front of 2,000 people to kick off a leadership weekend, and then two months later my wife wants out. My world was crushed!

I battled depression and questioned my reason for living, my purpose, and pretty much everything. I suddenly had to take care of a big home all by myself. At that moment, I realized one thing: Style with no life sucks and is completely empty. But the challenge was that we never truly had a solid home for our inner selves. I had to go on a journey that really hurt, but to discover my roots that were affecting my perspective of life, I needed to change. I had to dig into things from my upbringing that were never addressed.

That moment in my life reminded me of a tree that fell the other day in my backyard. It looked so good on the outside, but there were insects that you couldn't see eating away its inside and roots. And then out of nowhere—Bam! —it fell hard. Sometimes that fall hurts you and those around you, but you need to realize that if you had kept operating the same way, when a big storm came, you wouldn't last anyway. Another time, I had a tree fall close to the house and it crushed our trampoline. I went from being upset to being thankful because it missed the house by 15 feet. It was a workout to clean up, and we had firewood for a whole year because of it.

I had attitude and temper issues at times, and unfortunately, I took them out on the people I loved. Eventually, many of those people give up. It was Batman and Joker fighting inside of me, and I wanted Batman to win. That's why I say you must build your home first before going into the homes of others.

Marriage and relationships are about cherishing and about grace. We sometimes cherish our sports, friends, or even our car more than our spouse. But they are the most precious. You can like those things, but you can't love them. That's a dangerous spot, and I've been there. I cherish bonds and relationships so much more, now.

I was away in Vermont the other day, and I was sitting down while on my phone as some of the people at a nearby table were talking. One of the guys, someone I had just met and really liked, said to me, "Steve! Are those people on your phone here?" Right away, I put my phone on the table upside down, went to the table, and talked for two hours about life stories and laughed so hard. He was right.

"WE SOMETIMES NEED TO LEARN TO TURN OFF OUR ONLINE LIFE AND TURN ON OUR OFFLINE LIFE. BE PRESENT IN THE MOMENT."

We go to bed glued to our phones instead of glued to our partner sleeping next to us. Read the book The Five Love Languages by Gary Chapman. Quality time is a huge thing that women want. I'm no expert at this topic; I'm still learning. It's like the weather. It's unpredictable, but you need to do your best and go with the forecast and be prepared. There is no perfect way. Learn to be there for your spouse. Learn to ask, "How can I serve you or be better for you? What areas can I work on?" Also, it helps to be around a community of people who have great examples of marriages.

Also, stop allowing everyone to speak into your life; it's hurting your relationship. Learn to take advice from those who truly have fruit on their tree. Listen and read together so that you're on the same page. Love is kind and patient, so always remember that. It doesn't mean you need to be taken advantage of or tolerate abuse, but lead with your heart and be strong in a graceful way.

I write this because these were things, I wasn't doing all of the time. Sometimes, we get so caught up with "life," but at the end of the day, we realize it's empty with only style. I remember sitting in California a few months ago with my spiritual/

leadership counselor. We were talking about the word "lifestyle." Through our discussion, we decided that it's two separate words, not one.

You can have life with no style, and you can have style without any life. A great example of this was when my wife and I took a break, and she ended up leaving permanently. I lived in this great home, but it was empty. I had style but no life. What's interesting is that time in my life was actually the best thing that happened to me to help me discover myself. Silence and alone time may be the first time you ever get to truly know yourself. We know others very well, but we forget to take ourselves on a date and ask questions to get to know ourselves.

My "style" in life was actually covering up who I truly was. It was a mask, which I believe we all use at times. But when you have so many masks, you forget which one to put on that night you go out. That's an issue. With the word "lifestyle," it is truly life first then maybe style. Style by itself is empty. It's like winning a yacht but not being allowed to have anyone on it to enjoy it with you, which is pretty lonely and empty. Relationships are key and with the right people, such as your true friends, mentors, and spouse. Understand that friendships sometimes have seasons as well.

Everyone is going through his or her own issue, so stop getting so offended. Remember, love is not easily offended. We have all been there. "OMG, like Jessica never got back to me! It's been a week!" Stop it! You don't know what she's going through. Be there as much as you can, but don't take it personally. Stop being so sensitive. We have all been there.

"FORGIVENESS AND LOVE HEAL ALL
RELATIONSHIPS, NO MATTER WHAT THEY HAVE
BEEN THROUGH."

POWER OF WORDS

The power of words will either heal or wound those around you. In the Bible, it talks about how life and death are in the power of the tongue. I never realized how powerful those words are. In sports, we kind of just tossed them around, but in the real world, they can give you life or take you down. Whether it is in relationships with parents or with strangers, what is said to others is powerful.

Words are like scuff marks on a floor: if there are only a few, you don't really see them, but eventually, if you keep scuffing the floor, you will notice all the marks that have been caused from walking or dropping things. With people, you will see the brokenness that comes from being beaten down over the years by spouses, parents, or even coworkers. Words can create or destroy. The sounds that come from our mouth can be encouraging or discouraging, and the tone is equally important. Think about the difference between these two statements: "Babe, you never do anything around the house; what's the deal?" or "Babe, is there anything I can do to help around the house? I know you do a lot." There have been many times where I have spoken without thinking first. If your words could produce fruit, would they look rotten or be fruit that looks delicious? Learn to control the power of your tongue. We clean our house and our cars, but we also need to clean our hearts so that the right words come out.

"WORDS ARE LIKE THE WIND. SOME WINDS ARE WARM, AND SOME WINDS ARE COLD; SOME ARE STRONG, AND SOME ARE CALM. CHOOSE WHICH WINDS WILL MAKE YOUR WORDS INVITING TO OTHERS."

SELF-LOVE

The most important relationships you need to have, in my opinion, are with your higher power and yourself. Family, friends, and spouses will let you down, and sometimes we forget to have a relationship with ourselves, healthy self-love. I was listening to a story about CEO Charlie Jabaley (Look him up; it's a great story!) that talks about a story of him running, and on his body he wrote "self-love," and everyone started screaming it. He was over 300 lbs. and out of shape and lost 135 lbs. On the inside, he was dying and was unhealthy, unhappy, unfilled. He retired in 2017 at the age of 29 from both the music industry and the name CEO Charlie. He made the decision to reinvent his life in pursuit of his childhood dream to become an athlete. Charlie ran three marathons, became an Ironman, and even reversed his brain tumor. Even secured a partnership with Nike as an athlete. Going from where he was to the point of self-love was a huge defeat!

It encouraged him to finish the race. We love others, which is awesome, but we must never forget to love ourselves. If we take care of our neighbors' lawn but then forget about ours, that's an issue. It's very kind of you, but it goes back to the oxygen mask on the plane. Take care of yours first, so you can help others.

There are two types of love: imported and exported. The most important is exported love, which you give to others. If you rely only on imported love, which has to come from other things or people, there will come a time when it stops, and you will hit a wall. It happened to me, and it was not fun. I would seek approval from everything and everyone. It is not a strong spot to be in. When you focus on that internal love and respecting who you truly are, your exported love people will feel it. Then, you will naturally get imported love because of what you gave out. I call it "non-GMO imported love." It's not processed, and it's organic, so it's good to take in.

Those who become a magnet in life with their personality and vibe will attract people to them. People will sense the self-love you have and want to discover your identity. Sometimes, it is letting go of what you want and focusing on what you were created to do. Things will gravitate towards you without trying, just like a magnet. Not only will great people come into your life, but great things will start to happen and stick to your life.

I also think being able to be alone with yourself is important. Sometimes, we are so dependent on being with other people that it covers the faults we need to work on. We have become a generation that needs approval. I'm not saying it's not nice to get approval sometimes, but that approval has to come from you. It's like this book and the website I created. I prayed one night, and over the years, it's been on my heart to create Project Impact. The #1 approval was in my heart and spirit and my God to say, "Do it!"

DATING

I decided to put this part in here at the last minute because I always say to the guys I mentor who are single that if you want to find a great woman, you need to make sure you have three things in line:

1. Work hard to move out and live on your own.

2. Don't be an a-hole, but be strong with grace and love. (AKA like "The Rock")

3. Have vision, energy, and the desire to grow.

If you have those three things and smile, you will get the right person in no time. This works for women, also, and it's very attractive. The last tip to make this part simple is don't have bad breath. Have clean teeth, clean those ears, and guys, clean your neck hair. Also, be authentic and real. That's about it. Good luck finding the right person.

"CURRENTLY I'M DATING LIFE RIGHT NOW,
WE HAVE BEEN TOGETHER FOR 31 YEARS."

How Is Your Lawn

A relationship is like a lawn. It takes skill and time to let it grow and will sometimes look great and sometimes need fertilizer and water. Sometimes, you just need to plant a new lawn, which is getting new friends or starting the relationship over. Even the soil has to be changed to create the lawn you truly want, which means there are things you need to change inside of you like I had to. Remember, friends were once strangers. Never get turf, though. It looks nice, but it's fake, and people can tell. That goes for people as well. Look for real and authentic people. It's tough, but be around those who love you unconditionally not just conditionally.

I hope this gives you insight into relationships. It's a never-ending journey, just like trying to maintain a green lawn. You may think you have a grasp on it during early summer, but then something happens to make your grass brown or fade away. It's okay. Try watering it, fertilizing it, or planting new seeds. It can always come back some way if you want it. It will be with new grass that grows, and the beauty that comes from it will be all worth it.

"ONE SIDE OF THE WORLD IS WAITING FOR THE OTHER SIDE TO SAY HELLO."

QUIZ

Rate this Rock for yourself on a scale from 1–10.

_____

_____

What was your top take-away from this chapter?

_____

_____

What gaps do you have in this Rock?

_____

_____

What is your game plan and action to fix these gaps?

_____

_____

3

FINANCES

When you think about it, money is nothing more than paper that we say has value. Understanding the history of money is important so you understand that money is not made, it is something that flows to you based on the value you give to others. As soon as you stop providing value for your job, boss, clients, or society, that money stops flowing to you.

Many companies have gone out of business recently because they never adapted or updated their software to connect with the marketplace. Ten years ago, Nokia phones were the ones to have, and now they're gone. Toys "R" Us never made their stores an "experience" but were more like a warehouse of toys you could never play with and try but had to buy first. You need to experience things; they can't just be explained from a picture or instructions.

One thing I noticed in more affluent areas is there is no road rage or honking of horns. The reason is that they are usually not stressed about money because road rage is a byproduct of something else going on in someone else's life that causes them to get mad while driving. I remember moving into my area where I live now where people do very well financially. I was blocking traffic for about 30 seconds to get into a restaurant, and no one honked. No way would that happen where I grew up!

You will see people who have a good hand on their budget act calmer. Money is like air; when you don't have it, you panic and try to get more. I want to teach you the mindset of how to keep it and make more in whatever industry you are in. It's all about creating financial consistency so money doesn't own you.

HISTORY OF MONEY

Bartering was the way we exchanged services or products. The earliest forms of barter were cattle, sheep, vegetables, and grain starting in about 9000 BC. In about 1100 BC in China, people started using small replicas of goods cast from bronze. King Alyattes from what is now part of Turkey created the first known currency in 600 BC. Coins changed into bank notes around 1661 AD. The first credit card to appear was in 1946. We started with barter, and now we have cryptocurrency as a potential new form of exchange.

Timeline of Money

- 1100 BC In China, people started using small replicas of goods cast from bronze

- 600 BC First official currency minted by King Alyattes of Lydia in Turkey

- 1250 AD The florin, a gold coin minted in Florence and used across Europe

- 1290 AD The ideas of Marco Polo borrowed from China introduced paper money to Europeans

- 1661 AD First bank notes in Sweden

- 1860 AD Western Union, money with electronic funds via telegram

- 1946 AD John Biggins invented the "Charge-It" card, the first credit card

- 1999 AD European banks began offering mobile banking with smartphones

- 2008 AD Contactless payment cards were issued in the UK for the first time

- 2014 AD Apple Pay, Barclay, wristbands, blockchain

If money evolves through the years as it has in this timeline, you need to make sure the way you're making it also evolves. Many people who never went digital and stayed in the Yellow Pages never made it in business by not using Google. We make decisions in today's world based on reviews, and the Yellow Pages had to evolve as well. (As a kid, I remember getting those tossed in our driveway. So many trees were cut down because of those things. Did anyone else try to rip one up? The world's strongest men did it, so I tried but with no success.)

There are 14 areas I cover in this chapter:

- Act Your Salary
- Proper Budget Systems
- Spending vs. Investing
- My Bucks Vs. Starbucks
- Paying Off Debt
- Credit Cards
- Mortgages
- Savings Vs. Investing
- Retirement
- 50-20-30 Rule
- Active Income Vs. Passive Income
- Rent Vs. Own
- Asset Vs. Liability
- Taxes

These areas are key elements to putting yourself into a great position and never letting money control you or your life. Money is 80% behavior and 20% knowledge. It's our actions that hurt us. I hope the knowledge you learn in this chapter gives you a foundation in understanding the money game. At any time, our behavior can overtake our knowledge.

Unfortunately, our school system never teaches these areas, so I'm excited to get into detail and share this with you.

ACT YOUR SALARY

In today's world, we live in a society where we try to keep up with each other. My friend one time said, "Social media is eight to ten hours of people competing against each other for whose life is better and who owns more." How true is that! We grow up needing to have the newest phone, shoes, car, clothes, etc. It's fine if you can afford it, but really it comes down to priorities. I like to call it "phantom success" because it looks nice, but it's not real. We can get caught in this competition, and the person who loses is you. You see people with $100,000 cars who might live in small apartments or are still living with their parents. Everything in life can be fixed, including your spending habits and the amount of money you have.

If you lose it, you can always get it back. Its only paper, and you need to learn how to make it flow to you based on the value you give to society. Stop giving value, and money will stop flowing to you. Learn how to accept your salary. I speak about this in "Income Streams" where what you choose vehicle-wise will restrict the amount you're allowed to spend without getting into debt.

I remember when I was 24 and moved into my first home and got the first oil bill for $967. I wasn't sure if it was the rent or the oil bill! My dad always said if you want a big boy or big girl life (meaning an adult) be prepared to pay big boy or big girl bills. At the same time, these bills can sometimes motivate you to get off your butt and start crushing it in the working and money game. We can get too complacent in our lives so then we're not forced to thrive and accomplish more.

Wanting to make more money is not the question; the question is how or what desire do people have and what things do they not have that they truly want? Sometimes, pressure pushes people to grow, and it overwhelms people. Learning not to live above your means is important, but it can also force you to get out and kick ass. Anthony Robbins tells the story about a home he moved into that forced him to dream big and work his butt off. (I think he's doing okay, now.) But complacency can keep you in the same spot.

Not trying to keep up with everyone is a key thing to acting your salary. I remember when I was 23 years old, I was driving a Chevy Equinox with 18-inch chrome rims. That thing was hot at that time! I won "best car" at my high school with it. I went to a meeting with someone older, and he saw me drive into Starbucks. We sat down and spoke business and one of the first things he asked me was how I was going to talk about business when I was driving a Chevy Equinox. I looked at him and said "It's not about the car you drive; it's about what's in your bank accounts. Do you want to compare?" At that age, I had a good amount of money put away, especially with living at home, not spending like crazy, and my business was really thriving. He respected my answer and got the point.

Understand this, it's not easy nor healthy to try to keep up with everyone. You need to keep up with your desires and goals. Learning to stay in your lane is important. You see people going on vacation all the time when they still have debt. That's their choice, but it is different when you go on vacation with no debt and with money in the bank. I feel people go away, not to vacation, but to run away from their problems or debt. They can't afford it, yet do it anyway. They develop a mentality of entitlement saying "I deserve this."

"LEARN TO BUILD A LIFE THAT'S SO GOOD THAT YOU DON'T NEED A VACATION TO GET AWAY FROM IT."

It is important to be smart and understand what your current income is capable of. Create a good budget for you with someone who has fruit in this area of life to help give you a game plan. If you're not a mechanic, don't try to fix your car by yourself; learn from someone who has done it.

PROPER BUDGETING SYSTEMS

Pay yourself
Pay your business/asset
Pay your debts
Pay savings/investing

The reason why it goes in this order is that your income has to go to you first with what you get paid every month. This varies for each person because if someone doesn't have savings, they may not be ready to pay debt or start a business yet. I speak about having that extra cushion put away, but the reason why you pay your assets first before debts and savings is that it will produce a bigger return potentially and help you out-earn the problem. If you want to survive and not thrive, then paying your business/asset won't matter. Everyone is a little different, but these four areas are important to understand and know.

There is so much information out there, but I believe we don't want only information, we want truth. Systems are geared to make things work properly, so you must have one in place for income that flows to you. There are different methods to follow, such as zero-based budgeting. The main elements to understand are:

- Income/salary

- Fixed expenses

- Variable

- Business cost (If applicable to you)

Income is simple, that's whatever you take home after taxes, whatever cash flow you receive every week, bi-weekly, or monthly. Fixed expenses are things that don't change and must be paid such as cars, insurance, gym, electric, rent, etc. Be specific. Variable budgeting items are where many people lose money. These items vary based on your spending habits and lifestyle choices. The main variable expenses that you do need are gas and food.

Everything after that is a choice, including gifts, shopping, and going out to eat. Some of you might think, *Well, then how do we live?* That depends on two factors: your goals and your salary. Unless you want credit card debt, you must control your behavior. When your income comes in, your money will flow to fixed items then to variable items. Your goal is to make your fixed expenses as low as possible so you can then choose to spend or save/invest that extra money left over.

"A HAPPY LIFE IS A VARIABLE TO YOU. IT IS YOURS IF YOU WANT IT."

After figuring out what's left over, some of it goes to gas and then food. I recommend eating home as much as possible so you don't waste more money. That's a huge area where people lose their money in which they are careless in spending. The average household spends over $1,100 a year on coffee. Did you know that they invented a coffee maker in 1905 in Italy by Melitta Bentz. You can even have one at your house. It's amazing! Other things that people spend too much money on and don't realize are subscriptions that they don't use or cable television that they never watch or clothes that they don't need. All of the money that is not spent can go into:

- Paying off debt

- Investing in business/assets

- Savings

It's your choice where you want your money to flow; no one should judge you except yourself. It's about making good decisions daily, especially with the variable expenses. I remember as a kid getting lunch money for school three to four days a week, and I never spent it. I would bring food from home or eat someone else's lunch, and one day my parents found $1,500 in my closet. I had saved and been frugal with my money. Doing that as an adult in a society that is always competing will make you feel even better. Having money in the right places is like having heat or AC when it's cold or hot outside. It makes the inside of your home comfortable so that you enjoy it. When you budget with a proper system, you feel good knowing it's not taking away your focus or happiness.

SPENDING VS. INVESTING

Everything you buy or do is a spending habit or an investment habit. You will either lose money or get a return back for that exchange. A great example I heard was when Grant Cardone sat behind home plate at the World Series with a 10x hat on, which is his brand. Although it cost $40,000 for both tickets, he was able to write it off and market his brand on TV and social media for 3 hours in front of millions of people. That game lasted 18 innings, which made it a great investment! Another person went to the same game who invested $3,000 for tickets. Meanwhile, he was in debt and working a lot. That's spending with no return.

It's about getting leverage out of what you do, meaning how far will that money or time go that you invest. Since we have a limited amount of time in this life, we need to make the most out of it. People are willing to invest in entertainment yet they won't in self-improvement, health, or mindset, and then they wonder why they never progress the way they want. Traveling is something I get to enjoy a lot because of the international ecommerce business I built. I like to go to areas where I can do business and make the most of my time, such as seeing things or connecting with great people. Personally, I don't like just sitting on a beach doing nothing; I like to be on the go or working from the beach. Yes, it is nice to chill and hang out, but I love thriving in life. And if you are reading this book, I know you do as well.

Audit every decision you make and ask if it makes sense. I have a "5 Reason Theory" I came up with. If you cannot come up with 5 valid reasons that produce a return for why you should do or buy something, then don't invest in it. For example, say you have an iPhone that is two versions old, but you want the new one. If upgrading to a new one doesn't change your life or business, then why do it? But if the new phone will allow you to have more room to store content, a better camera for pictures for your brand, better videos, more apps to save time or money, and a quicker response time, then it might make sense. It was an investment decision, not a spending decision. People will buy cars or homes to rent when they aren't using them, and they make their spending decision an investment decision. Uber saw a gap in the world for cars not being used while people were at home. They asked themselves how to make cars an asset for people which would lead to them making money. Uber also created more of an efficient "taxi" system that has helped many people move around. They turned dead money into moving money and a service.

Even hiring landscaping or cleaning companies for your home can be an investment or spending. If you have a business or ways to make money, it may make sense to hire someone to take care of it this way you can leverage your time making more. We can all clean our cars, but we go to the car wash so that we save time and stress. This is leverage. When you buy a book, you spend the money to get a return on the knowledge you obtain. If you buy a book or magazine that gossips and teaches you nothing, then you spent instead of investing. You received nothing in return except negative news. Are you making more spending moves or investment moves?

"MASTER MONEY OR MONEY WILL MASTER YOU."

MY BUCKS VS. STARBUCKS

There are many different programs or business models that pay you a discount for being loyal users of their product or service. Many credit cards reward you in points or websites that give you a discount since they remove the middle man, and money flows back to you in different ways. For travel, including hotels and airlines, are there any programs or cards that give you free stays or rewards and also fits your budget? If you own a Mercedes dealership, why buy something at Audi and represent a brand that doesn't pay you? Learn to be loyal to what's loyal to your family. You won't see Lebron James wearing a Cleveland Cavaliers jersey while he is playing for Los Angeles Lakers. Derek Jeter, was loyal to who was loyal to him, which is why I respected him so much. He learned to win on the team he was planted with, which is why he was known as "The Captain."

Learn how to make your own coffee. If you buy Starbucks every day, and you are already in debt, then you can't afford it. I know it's a drug, and you like that cup with the mermaid on it and staying in a drive-thru line because you're too lazy to get out of your car, but you need to act your salary. All of this discretionary spending adds up. In 2017, the average person spent $1,100 per year on take-out coffee. Here is a tip: In 1908, Melitta Bentz created the first drip brew paper coffee maker using a filter she made out of blotting paper. It's dead simple to use and could save you a lot of money. Some may say well it saves "time" but in the end you still wait in line and spend extra money. Wake up earlier to get your day going and make good money saving decisions.

If you're always tired, then eat better and strive for a big dream; that will be the best and most natural way to get more energy.

Paying Debt

I think it's crazy how our college school system teaches us that it's okay to get into debt with an 8 to 12% interest rate. You get out of college with loans that are similar to car loans or even mortgages with no concept of how much they will truly cost. I will explain how credit card interest works and how to pay it off properly. Everyone is different with their own game plan and what makes sense to them based on what money they have saved, their income, or what kind of debt they have. It's important to have an emergency fund of at least three months of fixed expenses in case something happens. Once you have that, then you need to set up a game plan of how to pay off your debt based on your budget. Raise your income as high as possible and lower your expenses as low as possible. Learn to trim the fat, such as canceling memberships or subscriptions you don't need, lowering your car insurance, or buying less expensive groceries. This frees up more money to invest, save, or pay off debt.

Next, you need to determine which credit cards should be paid off first. There are great credit repair programs out there that also help if you have a lot of debt. Everyone's game plan is unique.

Meet Bob; this is his budget:

Income: $2,800/month ($700/week)
Total Fixed Expenses $1,900/month ($475/week)
Variable Expense $400/month ($100/week)

Credit Debt
Card 1: $1,200 at 28% interest
Card 2: $500 at 15% interest

Current Savings
$2,700

This leaves Bob with $500/month ($125/week) left over. Bob says he doesn't see that extra money and wonders where it goes. It goes into variable expenses because we just swipe that card and never really feel the money leaving our pockets. That's how credit card debt accumulates. If Bob sticks to his budget, he should be able to pay off his debts in four to five months, and then he won't have credit card debt anymore. It makes sense to pay the card with the higher interest first since your payments have more effect and save you more money. He has money in savings, but it's not equal to three months of fixed expenses. He could continue to save, but he will be wasting more money on interest every month, so for Bob, it might make sense to pay off his credit cards first, then start working on his savings.

Credit Cards

With credit cards, if you have a balance of $1,000 and your interest rate (APR) is 20%, the way your minimum payment is usually calculated is 1% is principal, which is $10 for the month, and the 20% is broken down in 12 months so its 1.6%. So that's $16 in interest you pay. Do you see the challenge here? You just paid more interest than principal so it will take years to pay off your credit card. That's why it's so important to budget correctly with a system to quickly pay off any debts so you don't waste money.

Credit cards should be used as debit cards, meaning that if you don't have it, don't spend it. Act your salary. There are great rewards and perks for some cards, so if you use your card for bills or business expenses, it makes sense to collect those points that turn into money.

Do you want to know where that "points money" comes from? When you use your card for business, they charge a certain percentage, say 2–4% for that business to allow that card to make purchases there. Half of that percentage will go to pay for the transaction, and the other half goes into the points/rewards program. You can thank your local business owner for the points you earned to go on your next vacation.

MORTGAGES

A mortgage is a loan from a bank or lender to finance the purchase of your home. When you take out a mortgage, you agree that lender has the right to take your property if you fail to repay the money you've borrowed including the interest. The home is used as collateral. Say your home is $300,000, property tax is $3,000 a year, insurance is $1,500 a year, your interest rate is 4.5%, and your monthly payment is $1,520. How much of that monthly payment goes to pay interest and how goes to pay toward the principal? Check out this table:

Interest – Principal
Year 1: $1,125 – $395
Year 5: $1,025 – $495
Year 10: $901 – $619
Year 14: $760 – $760

Not until 14 years later will you finally start paying more principal than interest. But then they will call you and ask if you want to refinance, which will restart the interest cycle. Lack of financial education means you will get taken advantage of. You should only buy what you can afford based on your income, and try to make double payments. If you paid off your loan on the bank's schedule of 30 years, you would have paid $247,220 in interest for that home. Think of how much you could have made if you had invested that $247,220 in stocks, real estate, or business.

Often, interest is tax deductible. This helps with potential tax advantages and incentives. Everyone's situation is different so it may or may not make sense to pay off your home right away. It's important to have someone to help you understand the financial implications. You might be able to make more by investing that money elsewhere than applying it to your monthly payments. Again, you need to sit down with an expert to see what makes sense for you.

SAVINGS VS. INVESTING

Interest rates on savings accounts have changed drastically in the past 30 years. In 1980, the savings interest rate was 13.5%, and today it is around 2.1%. In 1980, $10,000 would earn $1,350/year in interest; today it earns $210/year. That's a big difference. What's crazy is that banks are making a lot more money from your money than you are. They lend it to other customers for credit for homes, cards, or cars. The best deal in town is to own the bank. Use money that you didn't work for to loan to others.

Interesting concept. Don't forget to factor inflation and how costs increase every year.

- Gas was $1.06 in 1990 and is $2.49 in 2019.

- A new car in 1990 was $9,437 and $34,000 in 2019

- Homes were $149,800 in 1990, and in 2019, the average home is $274,000.

When your money just sits there and isn't invested, it actually loses value. Learning how to get a return on your money is key to keeping up with inflation. There are fiduciaries that legally have to give you advice that benefits you not just them. This will allow you to get returns anywhere between 4–12% or more. A basic Vanguard account in the S&P 500 has produced an average return of 9.8% over the past 90 years. That's a lot better than 2% from your savings account. When you invest in stocks, it's about how much risk and reward you handle and if you want to manage it or have someone else manage it. There are many options, so choose what you feel is best both relationship-wise and for the outcome you desire. Warren Buffet said:

> "If you don't learn how to make money while you sleep, you will work until you die."

> "Wall Street is the only place that people ride to in a Rolls Royce to get advice from those who take the subway."

You need to be aware of when you are spending vs. truly investing. It comes down to two things:

1. Budgeting correctly

2. Making sure your behaviors match up to your long-term financial goals

If those two things are in line, you will do very well.

RETIREMENT

Many think retirement is an age, but it's not. It's either:

- Steady income whether you work or not, like winning the lotto for life but actually earning it

- Having enough savings to live off of

- Having a pension that your company gives you

Now, depending on the vehicle you choose, this may happen in your 20s, 30s, 40s, or not till you're in your 60s or later. You get to choose when you want to retire from chasing money every day and start chasing goals and passions. I never knew I liked writing so much, but because I built a pipeline income that pays me well, it has given me the time to write this book and also do what I love, which is to mentor others in business and life. When you break down how you spend your time:

- 1/3 sleeping

- 1/3 working

- 1/3 living or doing errands

You get to choose when you want to make 2/3 of your life living and how much money you'll need to allow you to live that life you truly enjoy. But even when you retire from work or your business, you better have purpose or a desire for impact because only living for pleasure for yourself will get old very quickly. I like to golf, but I can't imagine playing that every day without getting bored. Don't wait your whole life to retire. Figure out ways that allow you to enjoy your life now and have options in your 30s, 40s, or 50s to travel, give to charities, buy that car you've always wanted, or take care of your family. There are many options; you only need to seek out knowledge.

Life is like a lawn; when you cut the grass, you know you will eventually need to cut it again. If you don't maintain it, you will lose the beauty of the grass. It is the same with your money, retirement, or investments. You need to monitor it. It's not just about making the money; it's about "maintaining" the money and then making it grow. You can let it sit there or make it multiply in many ways depending upon what value you bring to society and what your goals are. What's amazing is that one day that money you put away will help your kids or go to charities or wherever you want to help the most. Yes, you want to enjoy it, but also what you leave behind will be appreciated, and lives may even be saved because of it.

"A SOCIETY GROWS GREAT WHEN OLD MEN
PLANT TREES WHOSE SHADE THEY KNOW
THEY SHALL NEVER SIT IN."
—GREEK PROVERB

50-20-30 RULE

This is how you should divvy out your money that comes in.

50% is for your needs

- Groceries

- Housing

- Utilities

- Health insurance

- Car payment

30% is for your wants

- Shopping

- Dining

- Hobbies

20% is for your savings

- Savings and investments

This balance is key to being well rounded with where and how your money flows. It is a great guideline to follow to organize your money into the right places. Often, people struggle with savings because they don't have a long-term goal. Imagine if I told you to save $100,000 in 3 years and that you would win $1,000,000. How focused you would be! When you have a goal of where your money should go, then you are controlling your money instead of your money controlling you.

ACTIVE INCOME VS. PASSIVE INCOME

I speak about this in the income sources chapter. You can also call it bucket income or pipeline income. You will either have money work for you, or you will work for it. Go to the well to get water or create a pipeline that goes from the well to your home so it saves time and allows you to live life more. The reason why it's called active income is that you have to actively and continually work for it while passive income only requires doing something once and then it continually brings money in. There may be a little maintenance work required for that to happen, but it's a cash flow asset. Rental properties, subscription-based companies, or investments with monthly or annual returns are passive income streams.

"DON'T BE A HOSTAGE TO TIME OR MONEY."

RENT VS. OWN

This is case by case for each person depending on your income range and financial situation. When it comes down to cars, we all know that when you buy a new one, it depreciates as soon as it's driven off the lot. In the first 12 months, a car will depreciate by about 20%, so you lose a lot of money right away. If you want to buy a car that is also a good deal, you should:

- Lease one (if you don't go over mileage requirement)

- Buy one that is 1–2 years old, is in good condition, and has low mileage

A car, like your home, is not an asset; it's a liability. The exceptions are if you use it for business or if it is an investment, such as an exotic or vintage car.

When you purchase a car, you will probably make monthly payments for five years. Let's do some math…

If you pay $30,000 and the interest rate is 3.5%, you will pay $2,745 in interest total. In five years, that car will be worth around $8,500. You paid $32,745 total for that car, which means that you lost $24,245 since its only worth $8,500 after five years. Lease programs are sometimes cheaper, and if you have a business, you can write off some or all of that cost.

When looking for cars, it's a decision based on what you want and what you can afford. Many people ask if they should get a new or used car. With used cars, you can find great deals, and I recommend cars under 20,000 miles or less and in great condition. When you start looking at cars with more miles, you might run into maintenance issues that can cost more in the long run. You may have spent less on that car with more miles, but you didn't save peace of mind. Check out this comparison of leasing vs. buying:

Potential benefits of leasing

- Lower down payment
- Lower monthly payments available
- Repairs typically covered by warranty
- No selling of car involved at end of lease
- Possible option of a new car every few years

Potential benefits of buying

- You own the car
- Choose the level of insurance coverage you want to pay for
- Modify car without fear of breaking contract
- No mileage limits
- Sell car any time (as long as you pay what you owe for the loan)

This also works for renting vs. buying a home. Even after your home is paid off, you are still paying taxes, maintenance, and utilities for the home. You are paying "rent" money forever to live in your home. Yes, you do start to acquire some equity in a home as you pay it off, but as we spoke about before, it may be years before you start paying more principal instead of interest. Audit what is best for you on these two topics with someone who knows your finances, but also educate yourself.

ASSET VS. LIABILITY

A home is a liability because you have to pay money instead of it paying you money as with a rental property. When you think about what is put into your home to maintain it every month, plus all of the interest that I showed you before, you are putting money into something that does not produce a return. You may say the price of the home will go up, but in today's market, that's not necessarily true.

A car is a liability, as well because you don't make money with it. Becoming an Uber driver might turn your car into an asset, but it also depreciates your car faster through wear and tear and increased miles.

For all purchasing decisions, ask yourself if you are buying an asset or a liability. Recently, I upgraded from a MacBook Air to a MacBook Pro because of the work I can perform on it plus the time I save through increased efficiency. We often make liability purchases that produce no return just to look good or to keep up with everyone else. Try only to buy assets that progress your life or business forward. That's what the thrivers do.

TAXES

The U.S. government collects income taxes, payroll taxes, sales taxes, and real estate taxes from individuals and companies. The government disburses the money, according to its budget, to the appropriate agency to use for purposes like national defense, social security, education, national parks, or government services like welfare.

What is taxable income?

There are two types of income subject to taxation: earned income and unearned income. Earned income includes:

- Salary

- Wages

- Tips

- Commissions

- Bonuses

- Unemployment benefits

- Sick pay

- Some noncash fringe benefits

Taxable unearned income includes:

- Interest

- Dividends

- Profit from the sale of assets

- Business and farm income

- Rent

- Royalties

- Gambling winnings

- Alimony

- It is possible to reduce taxable income by contributing to a retirement account like a 401(k) or an IRA.

Tax basics: What are acceptable deductions?

The government allows the deduction of some types of expenses from a person's adjusted gross income (gross income minus adjustments). A person can exclude some income from taxation by using a standard deduction amount determined by the government and a person's filing status or by itemizing certain types of expenses. Allowable itemized expenses include mortgage interest, state and local taxes, charitable contributions, and medical expenses.

In America, our tax system is set up for employees to pay the most compared to business. Businesses employ others and keep the economy going and growing. We have a progressive tax system in which those who make the most money pay the highest percent in taxes. Except for those who make most of their money buying and selling stocks; they pay about half the percentage that everyone else pays. Businesses are taxed differently than employees and are allowed to only pay taxes on their profits and not their incomes. Businesses are allowed to report profits to their stockholders but then report a different number entirely to the government when filling out their taxes. Sometimes, very large corporations pay absolutely no taxes at all.

Companies are taxed, though, and pay their share. They also employ people, which stimulates the economy. They may have a large amount of overhead to operate, so if they did not get tax incentives, they would lay off employees. This is usually what is happening when a company has to "downsize."

Companies are taxed differently than the average citizen. When a person makes money, they are taxed on a portion of their total income. There are ways that you can avoid some of these taxes depending on your situation. If you buy a house, for instance, you don't have to pay income taxes on the interest you pay the bank on your mortgage. There are actually dozens of ways to lower your tax rate, but most of them are so obscure that very few people even know about them. But businesses are not taxed on income at all; they're taxed only on profit. Business expenses are not taxed. People aren't allowed to write off their expenses in this fashion, but businesses are. There are many ways that businesses can claim that the money they make isn't really profit at all.

What this means is that people who earn wages pay a certain percentage of their income in taxes, but if you own a business, you legally have write-offs that employees don't have, such as your car, phone, part of your home, traveling, and meals. Research it, and it will open your eyes to the tax breaks you get from being an owner vs. an employee.

DREAM CAR CONCLUSION

In the Corvette Analogy, a guy one day went to his friend's house who had recently bought a Corvette. He asked his friend why he paid $70,000 for a car when there are so many kids starving in the world. His friend explained what it took to get that car to that price:

- The miners to get the materials for the car

- The labor and trucks to bring it to the factory to make parts

- The factory that would start to assemble the car

- The shipping company and boat that shipped it

- The truck/person who brought it to the car dealership

- The person who was behind a desk to help coordinate the shipment

- The car salesperson who sold the car

- The person who detailed it in the garage

- The finance person who checked your credit and prepared the loan

- The person who signed the papers to let you drive it off the lot

- The gas station you got gas from

- The mechanic who changed your oil

- The carwash you got before you showed up at your friend's house

I think you get the point. That money flowed to so many people to get to that price. It goes back to how our money has shifted and the history of the barter system. Welcome to our new world of how money operates. Money is a tool to purchase products or services, and that's about it. I've been at the place where I loved money, and it broke me down. Loving money starts to own your heart, which is not a good place to be in. Should you work hard and get nice things? Of course. I had some of the people I mentor in business recently get me two amazing gifts for my birthday: a beautiful globe of the world and a gorgeous yacht which says:

"LIFE IS A JOURNEY OF EXPERIENCES AND WHO YOU SHARE THEM WITH. ANYONE CAN HAVE PHYSICAL WEALTH BUT ASK, HOW IS YOUR EMOTIONAL WEALTH."

One of my goals is to buy a yacht in the next few years, but I'm not as excited about the actual yacht as I am about the conversations, relationships, and sight-seeing we can do on it. It's your own personal cruise line that you can take whenever you want. What I am really excited about is I want to do a "Kids Dream Day" a few times a year with kids who have had hard upbringings with maybe parents not being there for them or being in bad environments growing up. I want to let them experience life on the water with a great day of fun and food.

Experiences are, what changed my life, and we build a life resume of those experiences. Money allows experiences. This past summer, I rented a villa for my whole family down in Barbados. My family will never forget that, especially getting to see my mom dance to Pitbull while working out at 7:00 a.m. on a cliff overlooking the Atlantic Ocean. That was an amazing thing to see and made me tear up seeing my parents enjoying life so much.

What's interesting about that trip is that as we explored the island, we saw certain parts that were struggling, and it broke our hearts. The second to last day of our trip, I was sitting on the deck overlooking an amazing view. Something in my heart felt wrong, and I felt guilty sitting there enjoying it all. Yes, I worked hard to enjoy it, but I felt an urge to do something. We decided as a family to do random acts of kindness and show love for the island.

We went to a supermarket and loaded up three shopping carts of food. People looked at us stunned thinking there was a storm that they didn't know about. We went back to the home, and as a family, we put all of the food in bags. We drove around the island for three hours and passed those bags to random people and stopped by some churches. Yes, the beaches and sun were nice, but giving back when you have been given so much is the best blessing. What's even better is that one of my best friends and his son were on this trip, and to see his son experience this giving back put an imprint on his heart for life.

I said this to a great friend recently who was in business with me for a few years:

> *"I may not have been able to get a check from you every month with the business we were involved in together, but I got something even more valuable: a true friendship with you and your amazing wife. I am so proud of you becoming a dad. Your son is going to be blessed with both of you and the foundation you already have and are building upon. You inspire me, bud, and I learn from both your heart and smile that you bless the world with. Anything I can do for you or any advice I can give, I'm always here for you, buddy. I just wanted to let you know that. Have a great day!"*

Budgeting is about being a good steward of your money. It's about deferring consumption with things you don't really need that maybe others do. Act your salary and be a great steward of your money for you and your family. I have seen money break families, relationships, and people, and it's sad. Please don't let a piece of paper break a relationship because, when you compare them, a person is a lot more valuable than a piece of paper. Always remember that.

QUIZ

Rate this Rock for yourself on a scale from 1–10.

_____

_____

What was your top take-away from this chapter?

_____

_____

What gaps do you have in this Rock?

_____

_____

What is your game plan and action to fix these gaps?

_____

_____

4

HEALTH

If you were given one car for your whole life that you must cherish, use, and take care of, how would you treat it? Probably amazing, right? No eating or drinking inside, shower after using the gym, and no passing any smells to your neighbor in the car. You would keep it clean and make sure you got oil changes. If you would do that for a car, why would you not do that for your life? You get one body, so take care of it. With so much research out there, many people don't want information, they only want truth, and that's what my book is about. I'm giving you the best content in one place without having to search everywhere and get overwhelmed.

Your body is made of six parts:

- Skeleton

- Muscle

- Nerves

- Blood/veins

- Skin

- Soul/spirit

Your **skeleton** or bones are the foundation, like the foundation that a house is built on. The concrete creates the solid ground we need to build a home upon. If your skeleton is not strong, your muscles will not hold properly. Another good example is the body of a car; your skeleton are like the frame. If the frame of the car is not strong, it will not hold its weight. I go over this in the vitamin section and having proper nutrition to make sure your frame is healthy. Like a car, rust starts to form, which is weakness in the frame, and it doesn't allow the rest of the body to hold itself together. Wear and tear will happen naturally, but it can be prolonged if taken care of properly. With a house, if the proper wood is not used, and the right beams are not in the right places, the house will shift and develop cracks over the years because the foundation was not taken care of properly. The same thing applies to your bones.

Your **muscles**, if not worked out, will eventually weaken. They are like the sheetrock and wood panels inside your home that allow you to build upon them. Proper muscles allow you to have proper posture as well. In today's world, when we type, we may be at our desk sitting down in a slouched position, and this happens when our muscles or framework are not strong. That's why exercising your back is key.

Your **nerves** are your operating system, the computer program that allows everything to run efficiently. Your nerves are like the electricity in your home that powers the rest of your body. It's what gives energy to the rooms or parts of your body. If these connections are not done right, your body doesn't function, or it operates in pain. Have you ever turned a switch on, and it doesn't turn on, or another room does turn on? That's because the connections are off and not put together properly. You need to make adjustments to fix those things that are off.

Your **blood** is the water that allows you to live in your home. *Disease* and *life* are in the power of the blood. Without blood or water, you cannot live and will eventually die. What we breathe, consume, or take in is vital to our blood. I remember one time I saw a friend smoking and said, "Do you cherish your life?" The answer was yes. I said, "If you truly cherish your life, you wouldn't put poisons inside of your body." This person put that cigarette down and never smoked again. If you value something, you will cherish it, especially if you only have one of it like your body for the remainder of your life. Certain things you can have in moderation, like too much tuna increases your chance for mercury issues in your body but is also a great protein source. Another example is red wine is good in moderation, but it can thin your blood and cause issues as you get older.

Your **skin** is the outside part of your home. It's what protects you from bad weather. It's like the siding or trim on your home. This is the panel outside the home that keeps out the bad weather that would affect the inside of the home. If it's wet or not strong, it doesn't create a good base, and over time, collapses and falls. Taking proper care of your skin with the sun is important. The outside of your home may start to fade in areas because of exposure to sunlight. (They don't make sunscreen for homes, yet, but when they do, you should totally use that.) Depending on what part of the world our ancestors grew up in, certain skin types are more adaptable to sun exposure. You should figure that out with your doctor. Natural Vitamin D is great for you but in moderation. Sun is life, but too much of anything can be bad.

Your *soul and heart* are the interior of your home. It's the design when you walk in and the furniture. I call it the feng shui. It's the atmosphere people feel when they walk into your life. Your vibe affects your tribe. You can have all of the other five areas of your body great, but this one is what lets people stay around you. How do you work on this area of your body? Take care of those other five areas and focus on your spiritual and personal growth rocks. Those rocks will be the best designer for your body.

KNOWING YOUR GOALS

Knowing what your trying to accomplish is key to your health world. There are four fitness types people strive for:

- Maintenance

- Bulk

- Shred

- Athlete

Maintenance is more of a workout to keep your body from getting out of shape. It's going to the gym 2–4 times a week for 30–45 minutes to keep a decent amount of fat off and muscle on depending on what you do. I call it the type of workout that you're either talking or on your phone scrolling for half the workout. With this goal, you keep your body in decent shape.

Bulk is basically not being able to fit into your clothes any longer because your muscles are bigger. You lift a lot of weight to gain mass and size. We also call that "hunka bunka" in Long Island, NY; I'm not sure what your term is in your local area.

Shred is being at the body weight you're supposed to be at, but you are in 6 to 8-pack mode. This takes extreme dieting and consistent workouts with proper nutrition and training to make sure your physique is good.

I have been an **athlete** for most of my life, which is when you're in good shape, can move around and do very physical activities with no issues. With this type of fitness goal, your body is in shape but also agile and able to move quickly. You're most likely flexible as well and have great energy when doing simple things like house cleaning, yard work, or playing with the kids. This type of workout involves super setting (not taking breaks between sets) and cardio mixed in properly.

"WORKING OUT CAN'T BE A GOAL, IT HAS TO BE A PROMISE."

WORKOUTS

Working out is like running your car and driving it to keep it working. If you let it sit too long, it gets rusty, and the pipes develop leaks. Your muscles, ligaments, frame, and blood flow are affected by not doing some type of exercise and movement. Depending on what you are trying to accomplish body-wise, a great trainer will tell you the type of workouts and the amount of time needed or diet to accomplish that body type.

Exercise can protect you from disease, slim down your waist, and also extend your life. This is why it's one of the seven rocks of life. Understanding the right plan and knowledge about how to set up your exercise routine is key to making it part of your life. You need to know why you're working out, your motivation behind it. There are also tremendous benefits of exercising, including:

- **Slowing the aging process.** Aging muscles have trouble regenerating and have fewer and less efficient mitochondria, which produces the energy powerhouses of our cells. But exercise, especially when it's at high intensity, will increase the number and health of mitochondria.

- **Makes you happier.** Exercise can alleviate symptoms of depression and help you deal with stress and anxiety. Just getting up and walking around may make you feel happier.

- **Lengthens your lifespan.** Exercise has been connected time and again to reducing mortality rates. Some of the most interesting research comes from extensive analyses carried out at the Cooper Institute in Dallas showing that runners tend to live about three years longer than nonrunners. Every hour of running you do adds an estimated seven hours to your life expectancy. In many studies, running just five minutes a day helps with a longer life span. Plus, you feel better afterward.

- **Improves your body composition.** Most people gain fat as they get older; it's part of life. But lifting weights and eating a good diet have the opposite effect: They help you build muscle and lose fat, even if you're over 60 years old.

- **Boost your brain health.** Studies have shown that aerobic exercise protects your memory and helps shave off cognitive decline as you age.

- **Improves your microbiome.** Exercise can drastically increase the composition of the trillions of microbes that live in the gut, which may be one reason it strengthens the immune system, fights inflammation, and helps with weight control.

"I DON'T ALWAYS DO SIT-UPS, BUT WHEN I DO, I IMMEDIATELY CHECK IN THE MIRROR TO SEE IF MY SIX PACK HAS ARRIVED YET."

SET GOALS

Starting your exercise journey can be scary. As many as 65% of people who start an exercise program quit in 3–6 months. What's even scarier is that less than 5% of adults obtain the correct amount of regular exercise that is recommended. A good amount to aim for is 150 minutes a week of moderate-intense exercise and 75 minutes of vigorous exercise. What stops a lot of people from achieving this is they don't have a strategy. You need to make sure you don't climb a mountain too high when you're not ready because, if you push yourself too quickly, you will never go back up to ski. My dad did that one time and went skiing from the top without learning the basics. It took him hours to get down, and he hurt his knee. With working out, you need to pace yourself to build yourself up. Here are some key things to focus on:

- **Be Specific**. Set goals that have a certain number of days each week and a set amount of exercises and time. Three days a week is good to start out.

- **Short-Term Goals** Setting realistic goals is key. If you push too hard too quick, you will crash, get sore, and not go back to the gym that week. Minor accomplishments are good because they build your confidence level and belief.

- **Process Goals vs. Outcome Goals** On your fitness and exercise journey, enjoy the process, not the results. You need to marry the process (workouts), not the results the workouts produce right away. Things such as time on treadmill or amount of weight or reps you do are key to monitoring your goal.

- **Be Real With Goals** If you can only do 10 minutes on the treadmill and expect to be at 60 minutes by the end of the month, your goal may be too big. Pace yourself so you don't burn out. Pushups and sit-ups in the morning are a great way to get started with natural strength. Some of my best times of being in shape have been with basic exercises and consistency.

- **Be realistic**. If you have just started working out and can only do one set of 10 pushups, don't set a goal to do one set of 50 pushups within a month. Focus on getting to a set of 20 pushups in your first month, then work your way up to 30, 40, and then 50 pushups as time goes on.

Goal setting will decrease your chance of dropout tremendously since you have a focus and goals to achieve. You can't build a home without a blueprint so don't try to build your body and exercise routine without one. Putting your workouts on your calendar is helpful as well. Remember, it's part of your seven rocks. When people say they are busy, it's just a lack of organizing. Clear the clutter in your life. You will always feel better after working out. Wake up earlier or go to bed later, the sleep you lose will be made up with the energy you gain from working out. If you have time to take the trash out every week, then you have time to work out.

VITAMINS AND MINERALS

These two are like fertilizer for your body and mind. It gives that extra energy you need and makes you healthy and operate at full capacity. Vitamins and minerals are essential nutrients because they play hundreds of roles in our body. As with anything, you can take in too little or too much of these nutrients. Having a healthy diet is always the best way to get a sufficient number of vitamins and minerals you need in life.

Every day your body creates and produces new skin, muscle, and bone. Our red cells carry nutrients and oxygen throughout our body. It also sends signals to our organs with instructions to help sustain life. To do this, your body needs raw materials to make this happen, which includes about 30 vitamins, minerals, and dietary components that your body needs. Vitamins and minerals help our bodies heal and also makes our immune system stronger. They also convert food into energy and the raw materials needed to repair cell damage. They perform many roles that are vital to the show your body puts on.

Taking vitamins and minerals is like fertilizing your lawn. If you do not properly take care of your lawn, it will turn brown. If you don't get all of the vitamins and minerals your body needs, you'll become tired and worn out—and look like it, also. If you eat a healthy diet, you can get all of your vitamins and minerals from what you eat, but most people do not.

Proper diet and food are like putting the right oil in your car. If you don't, you will never operate at full capacity. Eat the proper foods at the proper time based on your body type.

MICRONUTRIENTS

Vitamins and minerals are often called micronutrients because your body needs only a small amount of them. Failing to get even those tiny doses, however, pretty much guarantees disease. Here are a few examples of diseases that are a result of vitamin deficiencies:

- **Scurvy.** Old-time sailors discovered that living for months without fresh fruit or vegetables—the main sources of vitamin C—causes bleeding gums and lack of energy.

- **Blindness.** In some developing countries, people still become blind from a deficiency of vitamin A.

- **Rickets.** A deficiency of vitamin D can cause rickets, a condition marked by soft, weak bones that will potentially lead to skeletal deformities such as bowed legs.

Partly to combat rickets, the U.S. has fortified milk with vitamin D since the 1930s.

Just as a lack of key micronutrients can cause substantial harm to your body, getting sufficient quantities can provide a substantial benefit. Some examples of these benefits:

- **Strong bones.** A combination of calcium, vitamin D, vitamin K, magnesium, and phosphorus protects your bones against fractures.

- **Prevents birth defects.** Taking folic acid supplements early in pregnancy helps prevent brain and spinal birth defects in offspring.

- **Healthy teeth.** The mineral fluoride not only helps bone formation but also keeps dental cavities from starting or worsening.

THE DIFFERENCE BETWEEN VITAMINS AND MINERALS

Although they are all considered micronutrients, vitamins and minerals differ in basic ways. Vitamins are organic and can be broken down by heat, air, or acid. Minerals are inorganic and hold on to their chemical structure.

So why does this matter? It means the minerals in soil and water easily find their way into your body through the plants, fish, animals, and fluids you consume. But it's tougher to shuttle vitamins from food and other sources into your body because cooking, storage, and simple exposure to air can deactivate these more fragile compounds.

A CLOSER LOOK AT WATER-SOLUBLE VITAMINS

Water-soluble vitamins are packed into the watery portions of the foods you eat. They are absorbed directly into the bloodstream as food is broken down during digestion or as supplements dissolve.

Because much of your body consists of water, many of the water-soluble vitamins circulate easily in your body. Your kidneys continuously regulate levels of water-soluble vitamins, shunting excesses out of the body in your urine.

Although water-soluble vitamins have many tasks in the body, one of the most important is helping to free the energy found in the food you eat. Others help keep tissues healthy. Here are some examples of how different vitamins help you maintain health:

- **Release energy.** Several B vitamins are key components of certain coenzymes (molecules that aid enzymes) that help release energy from food.

- **Produce energy.** Thiamin, riboflavin, niacin, pantothenic acid, and biotin engage in energy production.

- **Build proteins and cells.** Vitamins B6, B12, and folic acid metabolize amino acids (the building blocks of proteins) and help cells multiply.

- **Make collagen.** One of many roles played by vitamin C is to help make collagen, which knits together wounds, supports blood vessel walls, and forms a base for teeth and bones.

What they do

Together this vitamin quartet helps keep your eyes, skin, lungs, gastrointestinal tract, and nervous system in good repair. Here are some of the other essential roles these vitamins play:

- **Build bones.** Bone formation would be impossible without vitamins A, D, and K.

- **Protect vision.** Vitamin A also helps keep cells healthy and protects your vision.

- **Interact favorably.** Without vitamin E, your body would have difficulty absorbing and storing vitamin A.

- **Protect the body.** Vitamin E also acts as an antioxidant (a compound that helps protect the body against damage from unstable molecules).

Because fat-soluble vitamins are stored in your body for long periods, toxic levels can build up. This is most likely to happen if you take supplements. It's very rare to get too much of a vitamin just from food.

What they do

Trace minerals carry out a diverse set of tasks. Here are a few examples:

- Iron is best known for ferrying oxygen throughout the body.

- Fluoride strengthens bones and wards off tooth decay.

- Zinc helps blood clot, is essential for taste and smell, and bolsters the immune response.

- Copper helps form several enzymes, one of which assists with iron metabolism and the creation of hemoglobin, which carries oxygen in the blood.

The other trace minerals perform equally vital jobs, such as helping to block damage to body cells and forming parts of key enzymes or enhancing their activity.

A CLOSER LOOK AT ANTIOXIDANTS

Antioxidant is a catch-all term for any compound that can counteract unstable molecules such as free radicals that damage DNA, cell membranes, and other parts of cells.

Your body cells naturally produce plenty of antioxidants to put on patrol. The foods you eat—and, perhaps, some of the supplements you take—are another source of antioxidant compounds. Carotenoids (such as lycopene in tomatoes and lutein in kale) and flavonoids (such as anthocyanins in blueberries, quercetin in apples and onions, and catechins in green tea) are antioxidants.

FREE RADICALS MAY BE HARMFUL

Free radicals are a natural byproduct of energy metabolism and are also generated by ultraviolet rays, tobacco smoke, and air pollution. They lack a full complement of electrons, which makes them unstable, so they steal electrons from other molecules, damaging those molecules in the process.

Free radicals have a well-deserved reputation for causing cellular damage, but they can be helpful, too. When immune system cells muster to fight intruders, the oxygen they use spins off an army of free radicals that destroys viruses, bacteria, and damaged body cells in an oxidative burst. Vitamin C can then disarm the free radicals.

HOW ANTIOXIDANTS MAY HELP

Antioxidants are able to neutralize things that may take away from your body such as free radicals by giving up some of their own electrons. When a vitamin C or E molecule makes this sacrifice, it may allow a crucial protein, gene, or cell membrane to escape damage. This helps break a chain reaction that can affect many other cells.

"WHY IS GOING TO A ROCK CONCERT NOT CALLED GOING TO A MINERAL CONCERT?"

SLEEPING

Your nutrition intake is key to your sleep patterns. If you put the right minerals and vitamins in your body, it will help you get better rest and increase your energy. Also, healthy sleep habits will improve your quality of life. It is also called sleep hygiene. These are some key steps that help to maintain a great sleep pattern:

1. Have consistent sleep patterns. Sometimes getting too much sleep will throw off your sleep pattern.

2. Practice a relaxing bedtime ritual. Meditating or reading is useful. Having a TV in your bedroom will ruin your sleep. Also, being on your phone before you go to sleep hurts your rest. Relax your mind or even have a nice conversation with your partner about life.

3. If you can't sleep at night avoid napping during the day. Now, I love naps; it's my time to relax my brain and is a form of meditation for me. But too much sleep during the day can hurt your sleep pattern.

4. Shower to be clean before you go to bed. You will feel refreshed, plus smell better next to your partner.

5. Exercising will help you to sleep better. Vigorous workouts are great, and you go to bed at night feeling accomplished.

6. Make your bedroom clean and clutter free. You will breath better and also feel at ease there. Less is better. Put your clothes away. Also, set the thermostat in your bedroom to a cool 60 to 67-degree temperature.

7. Sleep on a comfortable mattress and pillow and make sure they're not past their life expectancy.

8. Avoid alcohol or heavy meals before you go to bed. Also, avoid news and bright lights. These things affect your sleep pattern.

"IF YOU INTERRUPT MY SLEEPING, BE CAREFUL BECAUSE I MAY BITE."

FATTY ACIDS

Fats are complex molecules composed of fatty acids and glycerol. Your body needs fats for growth and energy. It also uses them to synthesize hormones and other substances needed for your body's activities

Fats are the slowest source of energy but the most energy-efficient form of food. Each gram of fat provides about 9 calories, more than twice that supplied by proteins or carbohydrates. Because fats are such an efficient form of energy, the body stores any excess energy as fat. The body deposits excess fat in the abdomen (visceral fat) and under the skin (subcutaneous fat) to use when it needs more energy. The body may also deposit excess fat in blood vessels and within organs where it can block blood flow and damage organs, often causing serious disorders.

- Fat should be limited to less than about 28% of total daily calories (or fewer than 90 grams per day)

- Saturated fats should be limited to less than 8%

Eliminating trans fats is recommended. When possible, monounsaturated fats and polyunsaturated fats, particularly omega-3 fats, should be substituted for saturated fats and trans fats.

These are the three kinds of fat:

- Monounsaturated

- Polyunsaturated

- Saturated

Saturated fats are more likely to increase cholesterol levels and increase the risk of atherosclerosis, which is the build-up of fats, cholesterol, and other substances in and on the artery walls. Foods derived from animals usually contain saturated fats, which tend to be solid at room temperature. That's why when you cook meat you will see the leftover grease harden as it cools. Fats derived from plants commonly contain monounsaturated or polyunsaturated fatty acids, which tend to be liquid at room temperatures. Palm and coconut oil are exceptions as they contain more saturated fats than other plant oils.

Trans fats are a different category of fat. They are man-made, formed by adding hydrogen atoms (hydrogenation) to monounsaturated or polyunsaturated fatty acids. Fats may be partially or fully hydrogenated (or saturated with hydrogen atoms). In the United States, the main dietary source of trans fats is partially hydrogenated vegetable oils, present in many commercially prepared foods. This is one of the reasons we have more of an obesity issue in America compared to other parts of the world. Consuming trans fats may adversely affect cholesterol levels in the body and may contribute to the risk of atherosclerosis.

You need to think of your body as having pipes, and if you put the wrong substance down those pipes, it will get clogged. People with high cholesterol levels may need to reduce their total fat intake even more.

"I AM NOT FAT; I JUST LOVE MY MUSCLES
SO MUCH THAT I WANT TO PROTECT THEM
WITH FAT."

FATTY ACIDS

Where's the Fat?

Type of Fat	Sources
Monounsaturated	Avocado, olive, and peanut oils
	Peanut butter
Polyunsaturated	Canola, corn, soybean, sunflower, and many other liquid vegetable oils
Saturated	Meats, particularly beef
	Full-fat dairy products such as whole milk, butter, and cheese
	Coconut and palm oils
	Artificially hydrogenated vegetable oils
Omega-3 fatty acids	Flaxseed
	Lake trout and certain deep-sea fish, such as mackerel, salmon, herring, and tuna
	Green leafy vegetables
	Walnuts
Omega-6 fatty acids	Vegetable oils (including sunflower, safflower, corn, cottonseed, and soybean oils)
	Fish oils
	Egg yolks
Trans fats	Commercially baked foods, such as cookies, crackers, and doughnuts
	Some French fries and other fried foods
	Margarine
	Shortening
	Potato chips

MUSCLE

Everyone goes on a different journey with weight loss. There are many outcomes that you may see whether it be body composition, strength or energy levels. Sometimes you will see your weight go up and that is because muscle is denser than fat. Also, our body is about 60% water so depending on how much we have that can play a factor. During this time, you must focus on your workouts, diet, how you feel and look without worrying about results. Focus on the work, not just the outcome, and you will feel better through your fitness journey of gaining muscle.

Muscle is composed of long fibers tightly woven together. Fat, though, is made up of different sized droplets and some are fuller than others. They will connect with each other but will leave some empty space between. As you reduce your waistline, you may not see a huge change on the scale because your body is burning fat but building denser (and heavier) muscles. These are ideal percentages for muscle-to-fat ratios from the American Council on Exercise:

	Women	Men
Essential fat	10-13%	2-5%
Athletes	14-20%	6-13%
Fit individuals	21-24%	14-17%
Acceptable	25-31%	18-24%
Obese	>32%	>25%

The two types of fats are subcutaneous fat and visceral fat. Subcutaneous fat is the outer fat, such as belly fat. Visceral fat is usually around your organs. Current research shows that your fat mass is like an empty bag of water but is in fact metabolically active tissue that acts as an organ inside your body.

Too much visceral fat can lead to cardiovascular disease and type 2 diabetes. Working to reduce your fat mass can reduce the harmful effects this fat has on your body. Our bodies are amazing machines, but fat does not turn into muscle. A loss of muscles mass occurs at the same time that fat mass increases.

You need to measure your body weight properly to understand what your body is made of. Doing this can show how much of your body weight is muscle, fat, and water. Only relying on what the scale says does not explain why your weight is increasing or decreasing. Take time to measure and examine your weight the proper way.

"NO TIMES FOR GAMES, ONLY GAINS."

PROTEIN AND CARBS

Growing up in an Italian household, we ate a lot of carbs. If you didn't work out, though, you would be in trouble. I remember growing up going to my friend's house, and his mom would always cook pasta. She insisted that if I didn't eat, I was not allowed back, even if I just ate dinner at my house. I learned a lot about carbs (and cannoli) at a young age.

Timing, portion, and type of carbs are key to not allowing it to turn into fat. Whether or not carbs are bad for you depends on your lifestyle. If you are going to be inactive for the next few hours after you eat, then carbs are not good. They sit there and turn into fat since they are not being used for movement.

Carbohydrates, proteins, and fats supply 90% of the dry weight of the diet and 100% of its energy. All three provide energy (measured in calories), but the amount of energy in 1 gram (1/28 ounce) differs:

- 4 calories in a gram of carbohydrate or protein

- 9 calories in a gram of fat

These nutrients also differ in how quickly they supply energy. Carbohydrates are the quickest, and fats are the slowest.

Carbohydrates, proteins, and fats are digested in the intestine where they are broken down into their basic units:

- Carbohydrates into sugars

- Proteins into amino acids

- Fats into fatty acids and glycerol

The body uses these basic units to build substances it needs for growth, maintenance, and activity (including other carbohydrates, proteins, and fats).

CARBOHYDRATES

Depending on the size of the molecule, carbohydrates may be simple or complex.

- **Simple carbohydrates:** Various forms of sugar, such as glucose and sucrose (table sugar), are simple carbohydrates. They are small molecules, so they can be broken down and absorbed by the body quickly and are the quickest source of energy. They quickly increase the level of blood glucose (blood sugar). Fruits, dairy products, honey, and maple syrup contain large amounts of simple carbohydrates, which provide the sweet taste in most candies and cakes.

- **Complex carbohydrates:** These carbohydrates are composed of long strings of simple carbohydrates. Because complex carbohydrates are larger molecules than simple carbohydrates, they must be broken down into simple carbohydrates before they can be absorbed. Thus, they tend to provide energy to the body more slowly than simple carbohydrates but still more quickly than protein or fat. Because they are digested more slowly than simple carbohydrates, they are less likely to be converted to fat. They also increase blood sugar levels more slowly and to lower levels than simple carbohydrates but for a longer time. Complex carbohydrates include starches and fibers, such as wheat products, bread, pasta, beans, corn, or potatoes.

"I'VE BEEN ON A DIET FOR TWO WEEKS, AND ALL I'VE LOST IS 14 DAYS."

PROTEINS

The body needs protein to maintain and replace tissues and to function and grow. Protein is not usually used for energy. However, if the body is lacking and not getting enough calories from other nutrients or from the fat stored in the body, protein is used for energy. If more protein is consumed than is needed, the body breaks the protein down and stores its components as fat.

The body contains large amounts of protein. Protein is the main building block in the body and is the primary component of most cells. For example, muscle, connective tissues, and skin are all built of protein.

Adults need to eat about 60 grams of protein per day (0.8 grams per kilogram of weight or 10 to 15% of total calories). Adults who are trying to build muscle need slightly more. Children also need more because they are growing. People who limit calories to lose weight typically need a higher amount of protein to prevent loss of muscle while they are losing weight.

"I'VE GOT 99 PROBLEMS, AND PROTEIN AIN'T ONE."

Dopamine and Serotonin

These two neurotransmitters play a huge role in our daily lives. Let's start with dopamine, which plays a big role in motivation and reward in life. When you have worked hard to reach a goal and hit it, the feeling and satisfaction you get are amazing. You get that feeling because of a rush of dopamine. This can be good or bad depending on what gives you that rush. Engaging in social media can give you a sense of accomplishment via dopamine. It feels good but is not always productive and then leaves you empty when you never really accomplish anything from it besides a thumbs up on your picture.

Some main areas and symptoms of depression include:

- Low motivation

- Feeling helpless

- A loss of interest in things that used to interest you

Many experts believe these areas of life are linked to a gap in your dopamine system. It can also be triggered by long-term stress, pain, or trauma. I have found that this can be true, but having the right foundation in life and areas that you are working on can change your dopamine system over time. I've seen it in my life when I struggled with social media, approval addictions, or anxiety for things that I was not in control of. I redirected my focus to allow dopamine to happen at high rates with simple things such as appreciating the food I was eating, family time or just being out in nature.

It really all comes down to a focus of what you pay attention to that starts to own your life. It's like ADD, which many people may say they have. They even prescribe drugs to reduce its effects. I have seen in my life and others around me, and you can combat ADD by finding something to do that you truly enjoy. This is not always the case but many times we lose focus or passion of things that don't inspire us or capture our attention. Many times, a lack of ability to focus can simply be because the topic or person is boring the individual which causes them to lose interest.

"DOPAMINE PARALYZES YOUR BODY WHEN YOU SLEEP SO THAT YOU DON'T ACT OUT YOUR DREAMS."

Serotonin has been studied for years, especially the link between serotonin and depression. It used to be thought that depression was caused by low levels of serotonin, although this has turned out not to be the case. The main thing serotonin does is process your emotions, which can affect your overall mood. Sometimes the worst disease is the one that is created in our minds and body. We self-inflict ourselves with poison with our emotions and feelings.

"IT ALL BEGINS IN YOUR MIND. WHAT YOU GIVE POWER TO HAS POWER OVER YOU."

PRESCRIBING VS. PREVENTING

We are in a society that feels they need medicine to cure or fix everything negative. Yes, there are times where medicine does save lives, but I don't believe drugs are the solution to everything negative in our lives. For example, with myself and others who have battled depression or anxiety, we are often prescribed pills to cure our "issues." To "cure" myself, I just focused on the seven rocks of life to get myself out of it, and I also had great support from some amazing family and friends.

If you can't build a home by yourself, don't try to build a life by yourself. You need help, but that help is not always a drug. A few months ago, I was getting really sick on a ski trip, so I started taking more vitamins and vitamin C. Four days later, my body was fine and naturally fought off being sick. Again, that doesn't always happen, but I have trained my body and immune system to be strong and not rely only on prescription medications. They can make your body weaker. I've also seen how certain diets can actually reverse the process of disease. You can do research on that.

Your body is like grass. The soil is on the inside of you, which is key to growing it. The water is the food and drinks you consume. The fertilizer is the nutrients and minerals our body needs to grow properly and survive. If you only plant grass seeds and don't provide nutrients, the grass will grow but not be strong. We can also lose strength and energy. That's why if you lack energy it's because of the "fertilizer" you put into your body. If you put too many things into that grass, you can actually burn it, and it will start to look sick. Everyone is different, and prescription medicines can save lives, but look at your options first.

FOOD AND DRINK

Growing up, my dad loved to bring home food that was amazing and showed his heart in who he was. The challenge was that the food was never healthy. Recently, I was at my parents' house, and I was hungry. So, my mom went in the fridge and brought out stuffed chicken rolls with cheese and pizza. I looked at her, and she knew what was coming. Being that they both had health scares the past few years, I get upset because I care about them.

I said to my mom, "Would you bring cigarettes home for the family to have?" She said, "Of course, not!" I said, "Dad bringing home food like this is slowly killing you. I know he cares, but it needs to stop." She got the point.

What we put into our body is important, and that's why we need to understand what type of fuel we need to operate at our full potential. Do some research to understand what preservatives and other toxins are in much of our food.

A can of soda can have up to 40 grams of sugar in it; that's like consuming 10 sugar cubes in one drink. This turns into fat and clogged arteries and increases our likelihood to get type 2 diabetes. High levels of sugar place a lot of stress on the pancreas, potentially leaving it unable to keep up with the body's need for insulin. Drinking one or two sugary drinks per day increases your risk for type 2 diabetes by 25%.

Social media uses algorithms to determine what content we like to see so it can show us more of it. With eating and drinking, you unconsciously use an algorithm that causes you to buy more of what is enjoyable, even if it's bad for you. You need to update the algorithm of your diet if you are eating bad and become aware of what consumption is helping you or hurting you in your health rock.

"I AM SORRY FOR WHAT I SAID WHEN I
WAS HUNGRY."

MEDITATION

Meditation is something I recently started doing, and I'm amazed at how relaxing and liberating it is. Sometimes, our minds are racing so much that we never take time to hear what is around us. I've learned that an:

"ENLIGHTENED PERSON TRAVELS WITHOUT
MOVING BECAUSE THE EARTH MOVES AROUND
YOU, NOT YOU MOVING AROUND THE EARTH."

We are always on the go, and like a car, if you press the gas too hard and for too long, you will blow the engine. Learn to sit back and listen to what is around you. Meditation is an approach to train our mind, just like fitness is a way to train our body. It's funny the house I live in has a Buddha statue that was there when I moved in, and I will not move it for two reasons: 1) He looks so cool, and I love the Buddhist wisdom/culture and 2) I'm afraid Jumanji will happen in my backyard if I move it. I saw what happened to The Rock and Kevin Hart in that movie! So, it stays there, and I see it every day.

Our minds are sometimes so full and cluttered that we never empty the things we don't really need. It could be worrying over our job, relationship, home issues, or finances. We train ourselves at work or the gym but never train the most important thing we need, and that is our mind.

Our mind is by far the best computer in the world because it has created the computer in the first place. A lot of people ask where to start with meditation. The main thing is to focus on your breath. Studies have shown that taking only ten deep breaths that are controlled and relaxed in a quiet place can change your whole state of mind. Try it right now. Close your eyes and only focus on your breaths. This is called concentration meditation, and what I now realize is that I used to do this before games while playing baseball. I would run, stretch and had a routine before the game started to do concentration meditation on a small little pebble in the ground. I focused on that for a couple of minutes to train my mind and eyes. This helped me focus on seeing the baseball and hitting among other areas.

Other ways you can do this exercise is by staring at a candle flame, also called fire gazing. You can also close your eyes and listen to nature such as the waves at a beach. It puts you into a great state of mind.

You will refocus your thoughts onto a chosen object instead of having your mind wander everywhere randomly. Through this exercise, your concentration will improve, and peace in life will start to evolve because you are training your mind to do so.

As I write this book, I have to be in a certain environment that allows me to focus. I have my phone turned off because the outside world affects my internal thoughts, and they don't become pure in what I really feel or want. That's why many creators or writers will go into isolation to create music or go in the woods to create content that allows the universe to speak to them. Studies have shown that, with these approaches, the relaxation response has shown short-term and long-term benefits on our nervous system such as:

- Lower blood pressure

- Better blood flow

- Lower heart rate

- Less perspiration

- Less anxiety

- Less stress

- Deeper relaxation

The main objective in mediation is that there is no goal, only be present. The ultimate result of mediation is liberation of the mind attached from things we cannot control. These things can be external circumstances and strong internal feelings, such as the topics we spoke about throughout this book. The liberated or "enlightened" person that practices this exercise creates a calm mind and sense of inner harmony that ultimately creates true inner peace.

OIL CHANGES AND INSPECTIONS

We routinely take our cars to the mechanic to change the oil and to see if there is anything wrong. If you don't do this, you run into problems later on that cost you more! The same holds true with your body. You need to make sure you're putting in the right "oil" for your "engine" to run properly. You may want to go on a cleanse to clear your system out. Even donating blood can be good because your body regenerates new, stronger cells, plus you also give back and save lives.

"HAVING A CAR IS COOL UNTIL YOU HAVE TO GET AN OIL CHANGE OR AN INSPECTION OR REGISTRATION OR NEW TIRES OR PAY FOR GAS."

We get inspections for our vehicles, and you need to get an examination from your doctor to see how your body is doing. Its recommended to get one every couple of years. A lot of people say they don't want to know what's wrong with them, but that's like saying you don't want to know what's wrong with your car even though you can tell something needs to be fixed. So, you wait, and then the damage costs a lot more to fix. Why have a car last only five years when it could last twice as long? Take care of your body and do oil changes and inspections on it.

If you invest now, you will not run into as many issues later, plus you will save money and gain back years of your life. You can tell how someone drives based on how fast they go through their brake pads. Most likely, if you go through them quickly, you have a heavy foot and stop very short instead of rolling into your stops. When a doctor checks your blood pressure or other areas of your body, he can tell how you're driving your body through life. It can look good on the outside, but the inside is where it counts.

"TAKE CARE OF YOUR BODY; IT'S THE ONLY PLACE
YOU HAVE TO LIVE."
—JIM ROHN

In wrapping up, your mind and body must be connected like a car frame and its engine. You must take care of what is under the hood. Understand what kind of fuel goes into your car for it to properly function. We educate ourselves on sports or movies but never health, yet our bodies are much more important. We must cherish it and take care of it for it to operate at its fullest potential.

When you put the wrong gas in your car, it doesn't run as smoothly and burns more gas and gives you fewer miles per gallon. If you want your body to operate right, make sure you are putting in the right fuel. If you never read the manual for your car, you'll never know what gas or oil is used for it to work best. If you take care of your body, you'll have an amazing machine that lives for a long time and looks great in the road of life.

I want to share some of my favorite recipes. I have also included two recipes from a good friend of mine. Chris Algieri who is a former super lightweight World Champion American Professional Boxer & former two-time World Champion Kickboxer!!! He has a phenomenal book called *The Fighter's Kitchen* on Amazon that has 100 muscle building, fat burning recipes with meal plans to sculpt your body. Also, there is one special recipe I included that has been passed down in my family. You are allowed only to have this twice a year. That's it! It's my Nonna's (grandma) special cannoli recipe. You must diet and train for months before you have this. Enjoy!

QUIZ

Rate this Rock for yourself on a scale from 1–10.

_____

_____

What was your top take-away from this chapter?

_____

_____

What gaps do you have in this Rock?

_____

_____

What is your game plan and action to fix these gaps?

_____

_____

SPECIAL RECIPES

Chicken Balsamic

INGREDIENTS

1/2 c. balsamic vinegar

2 tbsp. honey

1 1/2 tbsp. whole-grain mustard

3 cloves garlic, minced

Kosher salt

Freshly ground black pepper

4 bone-in, skin-on chicken thighs

2 c. baby red potatoes, halved (quartered if large)

2 tbsp. sprigs fresh rosemary, plus 1 tbsp. chopped

2 tbsp. extra-virgin olive oil, divided

DIRECTIONS

1. Preheat oven to 425°. In a large bowl, combine balsamic vinegar, honey, mustard, and garlic and season with salt and pepper. Whisk until combined. Add chicken thighs and toss until fully coated. Transfer to the fridge to marinate, at least 20 minutes and up to 1 hour.

2. Meanwhile, prep potatoes: In a medium bowl, add potatoes and chopped rosemary and season with salt and pepper. Add 1 tablespoon oil and toss until combined. Set aside.

3. In a large ovenproof skillet over medium-high heat, heat remaining tablespoon oil. Add chicken and sear, skin side down, 2 minutes, then flip and sear 2 minutes more. Add potatoes, nestling them between chicken, and top with rosemary sprigs.

4. Transfer to the oven and bake until potatoes are tender and chicken is cooked through, 20 minutes. (If potatoes need longer to cook, transfer chicken to a cutting board to rest and continue cooking potatoes until tender.)

5. Serve chicken and potatoes with pan drippings.

BAKED GARLIC BUTTER SALMON

INGREDIENTS

1 large salmon fillet (about 3lb.)
Kosher salt
Freshly ground black pepper
2 lemons, thinly sliced
6 tbsp. butter, melted
2 tbsp. honey
3 cloves garlic, minced
1 tsp. chopped thyme leaves
1 tsp. dried oregano
Chopped fresh parsley, for garnish

DIRECTIONS

1. Preheat oven to 350°. Line a large rimmed baking sheet with foil and grease with cooking spray. To the center of the foil, lay lemon slices in an even layer.

2. Season both sides of the salmon with salt and pepper and place on top of lemon slices.

3. In a small bowl, whisk together butter, honey, garlic, thyme, and oregano. Pour over salmon

then fold up foil surrounding salmon. Bake until the salmon is cooked through, about 25 minutes. Switch the oven to broil, and broil for 2 minutes, or until the butter mixture has thickened.

4. Garnish with parsley before serving.

BLACK BEAN SWEET POTATO BURRITO BOWLS WITH RASPBERRY CHIPOTLE SAUCE

Savory black beans and garlic roasted sweet potatoes are dressed in lime juice and fresh cilantro and served with spicy raspberry chipotle sauce in these sweet and savory vegan sweet potato burrito bowls.

Course Entree
Prep Time 10 minutes
Cook Time 35 minutes
Total Time 45 minutes
Servings *2 -3*
Author Alissa

INGREDIENTS

For the Sweet Potato Burrito Bowls
1 medium sweet potato cut into 1-inch cubes
1/2 medium red onion sliced into strips
1 garlic clove minced
1 tbsp. olive oil
1 tsp. ground cumin
1/4 tsp. salt or to taste
1/4 tsp. pepper or to taste

1 cup cooked or canned black beans drained and rinsed

1/4 cup finely chopped fresh cilantro

1 tbsp. lime juice

For the Raspberry Chipotle Sauce

6 oz. raspberries fresh or frozen

1-2 chipotle peppers in adobo sauce finely chopped

1 garlic clove minced

2 tbsp. maple syrup

2 tbsp. water

For Serving

2 cups cooked rice

1/2 avocado sliced

INSTRUCTIONS

Make the Sweet Potato Burrito Bowls

1. Preheat oven to 400°. Toss sweet potato, onion, garlic, olive oil, cumin, salt and pepper together in roasting pan or oven-safe skillet. Bake until sweet potatoes are tender and lightly browned, about 30-35 minutes, flipping once or twice during baking.

2. Remove from oven and add beans, cilantro and lime juice. Flip a few times to distribute. Season with additional salt and pepper if needed.

Make the Raspberry Chipotle Sauce

1. Place all ingredients into medium saucepan and stir a few times. Place over medium heat and bring

to a simmer. Lower heat and allow to simmer 15 minutes, stirring and breaking up any large chunks of berries with a spoon, until mixture is thick and syrupy. Add a few more tablespoons of water if mixture becomes too thick.

Serve

1. Divide rice into bowls. Top with sweet potato mixture, raspberry chipotle sauce and avocado slices.

BISON SLIDERS - from *The Fighters Kitchen* by Chris from Algieri

INGREDIENTS

12 oz. (340 g) lean ground bison (85%)

1 large egg

½ cup oat bran

½ cup finely diced white onion

1 tsp. finely diced garlic

½ tsp. salt

½ tsp. ground black pepper

8 cracked wheat slider buns

4 slices sharp Cheddar cheese

1 medium tomato, sliced

1 medium red onion, sliced

4 dill cocktail pickles, sliced

4 tsp. ketchup

4 tsp. Dijon mustard

DIRECTIONS

1. Preheat the grill to medium.

2. In a bowl, combine the bison, egg, oat bran, onion, garlic, salt, and pepper. Shape the mixture into 8 patties, place on the grill, and cook until still slightly pink in the middle, about 5 minutes per side.

3. Cut each slice of cheese in half and place one on each patty for the last minute of cooking.

4. Remove the patties from the grill and place on buns. Add an equal amount of tomato slices, onion slices, pickle slices, ketchup, and mustard to each. Skewer with cocktail toothpicks and serve immediately.

AVOCADO & SWEET POTATO HASH -
from *The Fighters Kitchen* by Chris Algieri

INGREDIENTS

1 medium red onion, diced
1 jalapeño, deseeded and flesh sliced
1 tsp. red pepper flakes
2 medium sweet potatoes, cut into ¼-inch (.5 cm) cubes
salt and freshly ground black pepper
2 cups baby spinach
4 large eggs
1 medium avocado, sliced
1 tbsp. chopped fresh parsley

DIRECTIONS

1. Preheat the oven to broil. Spray a cast iron skillet with nonstick cooking spray.

2. Place the skillet on the stovetop over medium heat. Add the onion and jalapeño and sauté until the onion is translucent, about 5 to 7 minutes, stirring frequently. Stir in the red pepper flakes and transfer the mixture into a bowl.

3. Add the sweet potatoes to the still-hot skillet and season with salt and pepper. Cook until soft, about 8 to 10 minutes. Add the spinach and cook until wilted, about 1 to 2 minutes. Add the onion and jalapeño mixture back into the skillet and stir into the potatoes.

4. Crack each of the eggs on one-fourth of the mixture. Place the skillet in the oven and broil until the eggs are set, about 5 to 7 minutes.

5. Remove the hash from the oven, top with the avocado slices, sprinkle the parsley over the top, and serve immediately.

FAMOUS NONNA'S CANNOLI CRÈME RECIPE!

INGREDIENTS

3 lbs ricotta
4 cups milk
9 tbsp corn starch
1 cup sugar cinnamon

½ tsp vanilla extract
1 orange
1 lemon
Confectioners sugar
Chocolate morsels
Colored sprinkles

Pour cold milk into pot. Add 9 tablespoons of corn starch into milk and make sure it's dissolved. Add sugar, cinnamon, vanilla extract, orange peels, lemon peels, and stir mixture with a wooden spoon in a continuous stirring motion on medium heat. Continue stirring to boil until mixture thickens while lowering heat. Once mixture thickens, remove from stove and keep it cool for a couple of hours. Refrigerate.

After refrigeration, remove orange and lemon peels from prepared mixture. Alternate mixing corn starch mixture in strainer and add some ricotta and sugar and pass through strainer. Continue alternating corn starch mixture and sugar and ricotta through the strainer until all is used and place in bowl.

Stuff cannoli crème into cannoli shells with small spoon.

Optional: Add chocolates morsels or colored sprinkles on both ends and sprinkle with confectioners sugar.

5

INCOME STREAMS

Instead of asking young people what they want to be when they grow up, I think the right question is how do they truly want to live their life. When it comes to finances, what do you feel will fit your dreams and the outcome you desire? The reality is that our school systems, program us to be great at working a job, but rarely teaches how to have an entrepreneur mentality. John D. Rockefeller once said, "I don't want a nation of thinkers; I want a nation of workers." You can take that quote however you want, but it seems to reflect what our school system teaches. They encourage us to think one way and not truly think freely. If you have a lid on a jar filled with flies, they will learn that they can't go higher and stop before reaching the top. If you take the lid off, they still won't fly away because they are conditioned to stop. We also live with systems that put lids on us and limit our dreams and goals.

There are two types of lifestyles: surviving and thriving. Fortunately, you get to choose how you live. The paths you choose create the outcome you want. I remember being asked to rate my life on a scale of 1 to 10 in regards to time and money. I said -2. I was doing poorly as a college student, eating Taco Bell every other day, and had no money, only meal points on my school card. Then, I learned there were three things I needed to change to get the life I wanted:

1. Having a mentor

2. Educating yourself

3. Choosing the proper vehicle

We sometimes are "A" players in life, but we are stuck in this C or D game that doesn't allow us to create the best outcome for our family and ourselves. We have restrictions that stop us from living at our full potential. We too often try to be an artist in life without a producer (a mentor) helping us. The A players understand the power of a coach. You need to find a mentor who can help you get to that next level. It's that mentor/mentee relationship that will help you reach the success and goals you want. Find someone who has walked the same path so your trip is not so long or bumpy.

"A GREAT PRODUCER IN LIFE PRODUCES RESULTS. BE THAT ARTIST WHO IS WILLING TO LEARN SO EVENTUALLY YOU WILL BECOME THE PRODUCER FOR OTHERS."

I always say you cannot live a new life with old information. You need to reprogram and update your software to be relevant. Why would you listen to cassette players when you have Spotify or iTunes on your phone? Learn about topics you want to be successful at. Elon Musk learned rocket science by just studying it; he didn't go to school for it. Information is more available than ever before.

If I were to give you a Lamborghini or tug boat, which vehicle would you want? You might say you want the Lambo, but first you need to know what you need it for. If you need to move a barge, then a tug boat would be far more valuable.

Wealth can be broken down into two areas:

First, having a network, being an influencer, or having a service or product. Second, being able to provide value and answers to others. It's not about making money; it's about having money flow to you because of what you provide. Money flows to whoever has a better product or service, whoever provides the most value. You need to ask where you can provide the most value.

Here is a great example. Years ago, Blackberry and Nokia were crushing the cell phone game. They owned the market until along came a man named Steve Jobs that had the vision of making a phone called the iPhone. He created something that others did not see because people don't know what they want until they know what they can have. Money flowed from Nokia and Blackberry to the iPhone because it was something that provided better value. This happens all the time. Uber took business from taxi companies. In 2013, Medallions (permit in U.S. allowing taxi drivers to operate) used to cost $1.3 million; now they are worth $160,000. Learn how to make money flow to you based on what you provide that is better or different.

BUCKET OR PIPELINE

Entrepreneurship allows you to better control that flow of money. It's not as easy if you have a job because someone else places limits on what they think you are worth salary wise. It's not bad but restrictive. Most of the time, you need your job to supply some type of income on your journey into entrepreneurship, but then it's those after-hours or free time on weekends that allow you to create something else if you choose.

There are two types of income that I call Bucket Income and Pipeline Income. These are also known as active income and passive income. If you think about the word *income*, you must go *in* for it to *come* out. Pretty simple, right? If you were to build a sand castle by the ocean during low tide, you could build it with no issues. Two hours later, however, the high tide comes and washes all your work away. That's what active income is like because if you do not go *in to work for it*, it does not *come* out. The tide washes away your sand castle every few hours and the income during the week gets washed away also.

The true currency of life is not money but time, yet we consistently exchange our time for money because that's all we know. Ask yourself, "What is it that I currently don't have that I do want in my life." If something is lacking, then ask what you need to change. You might have to change your career, your income vehicle, or your mindset. If you're not satisfied with only surviving but instead want to thrive, ask questions like:

- What do I want in this life?

- When do I want those things?

- What am I willing to let go of to get them?

You'll notice this as well in the mindset of employees vs. entrepreneurs. Neither one is better than the other; it just depends on how you want to make money, think, and live your life. People who only have a "surviving" mentality watch TV a lot, are on social media a lot, and waste a lot of time every day. They often talk about the good old days but never create any new days. They complain about how things cost a lot but never figure out how to out-earn the issue. People who have a thriving mentality love learning, growing, and gaining content in life to make them better. There are employees and entrepreneurs on both sides of surviving and thriving. You need to choose how far and high you want to go. You want to have your "main gig" then your "side gigs" in life. Eventually those "side gigs" will be the main things you do and most likely things you truly enjoy. You may be at the point where you don't want the responsibility of owning a business or starting from scratch, and that's okay. It comes down to what you feel will fulfill your dreams and desires. A certain job may do that if the salary they pay you allows you to do what you want. I remember hearing one time that:

> "EVERY JOB YOU HAVE WILL PAY YOU A CERTAIN
> SALARY, AND THAT INCOME WILL RESTRICT
> THE DREAMS AND GOALS YOU DESIRE ALONG
> YOUR JOURNEY."

If you're a teacher, you may love being with kids and having your summers off. Awesome, keep doing that. If you work as a doctor, engineer, or accountant, you may love being able to save lives, design, or you are great with numbers. You can work on both at the same time if you want. You could work 9am–5pm to survive and then work 5pm–10pm on other projects to thrive and get to that next level or start your own business. It's your choice and something only you will know.

MINDSET

> "A GREAT MAN OR WOMAN CAN TAKE CARE
> OF ONE TO TWO GENERATIONS ABOVE AND
> BELOW THEM."

Do you feel you've reached your limit for achieving your dreams or increasing your income? If so, what needs to change? What shifted me toward being an entrepreneur was seeing my siblings go through so many jobs and getting laid off. That made me realize that working for someone else was the "architect" of my life that prevented me from reaching my destiny! I also saw my dad work in real estate where he was able to spend life with his family, not just leftovers after work but true quality time. We were very blessed to have our dad present in our lives and able to go to sports we played and be around us growing up. I used to think my dad was in the Mafia because we were Italian and he drove Cadillacs.

SURVIVE OR THRIVE

I want to talk about a few fundamentals to creating proper income or wealth. There is a surviving mentality vs. thriving mentality. Notice how surviving thinks smaller and thriving thinks bigger. Surviving believes money is earned through labor, whereas thriving believes it's earned through thought. Some people care about title or status and many of the thriving care about outcome, result, and impact on society. Bill Gates and Steve Jobs cared about building something that changed the world. They built systems instead of working for one, which allows you no limits to where you want to go. It's all mindset that restricts people from reaching that next level in life.

A surviving mentality will complain about problems, and a thriving mentality will come up with a solution to see how they can make it better or fix it. It's like trying to get a couch down a stairway when one person gets stuck. They get tired midway because the couch is not going anywhere. The thriver mentality took the time to think first about the angles and how to go down properly to save time and energy. They work less and are more efficient. Survivors will be on social media or watch Netflix, and thrivers will be reading, listening, or watching inspiring videos or documentaries. They do the mental homework to make sure they go through life most efficiently. They look at the stairs of life first, study the best way to go down, and then take massive action.

Look at how many people have come to America from their home countries where they were only surviving. They could have stayed there, but they decided to pack up and move into a foreign environment that would give them more opportunities for their family. They were not satisfied. Many people who have immigrated to America have a different focus and work ethic than those born in America. Their mindset when they come to this country has a mentality of, "We are going to thrive. That's it; no other choices!" They have nothing else to lean on. It's as if you had a tiger behind you and in front of you was a cliff with water far below. Do you stay and get eaten or do you jump? Learn to jump into a great mindset of success.

DUPLICATION

Learning to leverage or outsource will put you into a good financial position and also buy back some of your time. There are things you can do to save money by not hiring someone, whether it's landscaping, house cleaning, an oil change, or cleaning the pool. But you usually hire someone, and you're willing to pay because you may not know the craft well and don't have time to learn it. So, you use someone else, and it also saves time. This allows you to do other things that can make you even more money than you spend, especially when you own a business. If you don't learn this concept, a company will control your time. You won't own *it*; it will own you!

The challenge many face as an employee is not being able to afford to duplicate yourself. But duplicating yourself can give you a lot of leverage. Building systems and documenting them is the first step to duplicating yourself. You then teach those systems to someone else who can do them for you at a lower cost than what your time is worth.

TWO DIFFERENT AGES

As life moves forward, we forget to upgrade our software in many parts of our lives. Most people are operating on systems that are hopelessly outdated and don't function nearly as well as they should. We update our phones but forget to update ourselves to reflect how money and the marketplace are evolving. In today's world, what has previously taken years to create can now take only months or weeks. Look at how many companies are outsourcing to other parts of the world because it's cheaper and more efficient. Many times, our mindsets or the ways we make income are expired. We still try to use it, but it's not producing the effects it once had.

There are millions of websites filled with information to help you become more efficient in whatever you need. I grew up with encyclopedias (I honestly forgot how to spell that word while writing this), but now you can Google almost anything. But you need to be careful because the Internet often states opinions and anyone can put information there. You can also go to YouTube for information about anything such as how to fix something or ski or learn a new program on your computer. We used to go to the library when we needed information; now we go online.

The point is how are you making income in today's world. Look at Elon Musk creating the hyperloop and changing the way we travel. Our travel system with planes has not changed in decades. Nothing evolved until recently with the different projects Elon Musk and electric cars have started to do.

What is the best and most efficient way for you to fulfill your goals and dreams? There are different ways to work out, but we are all pushing toward the same results: healthy and in-shape bodies. Make sure you are not operating on software that expired years ago. It may still work, but it's not getting you through life effectively. With today's world and technology, we are also losing jobs for people because computers are taking over. Two great examples are E-ZPass tolls for vehicles and self-checkout counters at stores such as Home Depot. You need to keep up.

"SOME PEOPLE'S KNOWLEDGE OR MINDSET HAVE EXPIRED. MAKE SURE YOURS IS UP-TO-DATE!"

CIRCLE OF FRIENDS

I speak about this throughout the book, but I believe in this very much. You can't expect a tiger to feed his family when he has only been around little cats who take down mice for a living. There is a Spanish saying I learned from my friends down in Miami: "Las palabras se han ido con el viento," which means, "Words are taken by the wind." When you want to grow personally or start a business, you will have friends, family, or even strangers give you opinions that are "expired" and not valid. Let the wind take those words if they will not empower you along your journey.

That's why it's important to see if you're following surviving advice or thriving advice. Your environment is what makes you who you are. Being careful about who you surround yourself with so you can have a thriving life. When I was playing baseball at higher levels, it didn't make sense for me to be with lower talent because I would fall down to their level. My skills would decrease instead of increase. At the gym where I work out frequently, I have a friend who is 6' 5" and 270 pounds of muscle. As I write this, I'm still sore from a workout we had five days ago! He can yell at me anytime he wants because he is big and in shape. But if someone else tried that, someone with no results, I would tell them straight up, "Stop giving me expired advice that has no credibility." I would then smile and walk away.

Don't try to be in the majors when you're around minor league talent and mindsets. You can still be friends with those people, just make sure your time is limited if you have big goals and dreams to accomplish. But if you want to stay playing high school soccer and never make it to the MLS or FIFA pros, keep your same sphere of influence. I've learned that successful people are not always available people because they are in the process of using their time wisely.

The tribe you choose is very important, although it may adjust at times throughout your life. Your tribe affects your vibe, attitude, and dreams. You can't build an empire or become wealthy in isolation. You are only as good as the community that you surround yourself with and associate with. We can't be on islands by ourselves; we need great communities to help make that island livable.

"WHY WOULD YOU PLANT A SEED ON CONCRETE AND EXPECT IT TO GROW? PLANT YOURSELF IN SOIL TO GAIN UNDERSTANDING, AND YOU WILL START TO KNOW."

LIABILITY OR ASSET

Looking at the things you buy or the things you do is key to successfully knowing if it was a liability move or an asset move. I've done many liability moves in my life, such as buying a car, a watch, clothes, or anything else I didn't really need. We all have good taste, but sometimes our taste makes us live a liability life that's tight. Many think a home is an asset, but it's a liability because most homes we live in don't produce income. If you have tenants, then your building is an asset. If you have an office in your home, there are tax incentives for that, same for a car that is used for your business.

Every day we make liability or asset decisions, so learn which one will help you the most. We live in a society where everyone wants to buy the latest and greatest things. We don't know how to defer consumption with those things we truly don't need. I currently own an older model of iPhone, and although I can afford the latest one, why fix something that isn't broken? People do that with cars and clothes, also. These are liability decisions. Survivors will make liability decisions, and thrivers make asset decisions daily.

"SOME PEOPLE INVEST MORE IN THE WEEKEND THEN THEY DO IN THEIR FUTURES."

REAL SOCIETY EDUCATION

There are three types of education in today's world: scholar, professional, and financial. Let's start with scholar first.

I'm sure many of you have strong opinions about our education system. Many feel it's broken and out-dated, and some feel it's great. I've learned that you can't pay bills with grades; you must pay bills with money. I used to stress out a lot about doing badly on a test. I believe you should do well in school, and it helps to show your focus and work ethic. But I have seen C students who have ADD become owners of very successful companies and now those A students are working for them.

Many people use the ADD label. That happened to me as a kid when I was in 4th grade. I was told I was going to be left behind. My parents and I did not accept that, and I passed that year and never looked back, finishing my college career with a 3.8 GPA and a double major. Many people who are labeled as ADD are simply bored and whatever they are supposed to be paying attention to doesn't keep them focused.

Unfortunately, student loan debt is at an all-time high with interest rates between 3.4% and 8.5%. Kids are graduating with a mortgage but no home. When it comes to college, you need to ask if you are receiving a real-world education that is only applicable to society's current needs (which shift every day). After you graduate four years from now, the topic you learn about could become irrelevant in the marketplace. I sat in classes where I often wondered when I would ever use that information. I think sometimes we add things to our software or brains that don't need to be there when we really need to learn other things like budgeting, finances, or any of the other areas I speak about in this book. For certain careers, like doctors or engineers, go to school. I don't want to hear that my doctor learned medical procedures from YouTube.

Society is conditioned to think normal, not abnormal. They are conditioned to this one way and are in one box. Imagine if you grew up where all you got to see was that one small room you lived in with your parents. Simple life and very little knowledge. We live in metaphorical boxes and never explore other boxes that might have so much more to offer. We get comfortable in these boxes because we have been there for so long. But once you discover a bigger box, your mind is blown away, and you never want to go back to that limited box.

> "THE ILLITERATE OF THE 21ST CENTURY WILL
> NOT BE THOSE WHO CANNOT READ OR
> WRITE, BUT THOSE WHO CANNOT LEARN,
> UNLEARN, AND RELEARN."
> —ALVIN TOFFLER

PROFESSIONAL EDUCATION

What professional education does is program you to follow a system and not question anything. It sometimes doesn't allow you to think freely, depending on the field you study. Our school system and our job system are extremely similar.

- For one we use a bus, the other a car or train

- Both have lunch breaks

- One has a teacher, the other a boss

- One has homework, the other has paperwork

- One has days off, the other has time off

- In one you get paid with grades, in the other you get paid with money

- They both start in the morning and end later in the afternoon

You're programmed to be an employee, not a freelancer or entrepreneur, and that's okay if that's what you want. Education for doctors, lawyers, dentists, engineers, and accountants is considered professional education and follows certain protocols to be in those careers. Some great qualities that come from this education, like being on time, being accountable for your homework or paperwork, and how to learn from others.

Financial Knowledge

Financial education is something we never learn in school, unfortunately, or at least very rarely. I always wondered why we never learned about interest, bank accounts, investments, debt, and mortgages until we were out of school and in the real world where we have to quickly learn all of these new terms. We get older and the first and main thing we complain about is money. It's the thing that controls our mind, lives, and relationships. We never learn about short-term or long-term investments. Financial literacy is the possession of skills and knowledge that allows an individual to make informed and effective decisions with all of their financial resources. We never learn how to make informed decisions, which then puts our family in generational financial struggle. There are so many examples of families not just passing down money but passing down the wisdom of how to keep it and multiply it. We all know what Warren Buffet does, but what people miss is *how* he does it. The mindset behind his investments is priceless. If I could, I would pay for the mindset he has and the strategy of why he invests the way he does. Families that continue to pass down and create generational wealth do so mainly through proper financial education. *Knowing not just how to make money, but how to keep it while being great stewards of it and also learning how to make it multiply.*

"PROGRESS MAKES US HAPPY, NOT JUST MONEY,
BUT GET GREAT AT MAKING IT AND KEEPING IT."

LEADERSHIP

You need to be the leader of your own ship before you can be a captain to others. That's why personal growth is so important. At first, you will need to follow others until you feel comfortable with that role. John Maxwell is an amazing leadership coach who has spent decades studying teaching leadership. I recently had the privilege of meeting him.

There are two types of leaders: the travel agent and the tour guide. A travel agent will tell you where to go, and a tour guide will take you where you want to go. You can choose the type of leader you want to be, but the tour guide leaders connect more because they walk the path with you. They feel more secure, but eventually they will become so strong that you can be a travel agent to them. This is important in developing organizations, teams, or companies, and the leadership style you choose can create a culture that the right people will enjoy.

Many great leaders or CEOs feel that their employees come first, then their customers. If your employees are not taken care of, then your customers will feel it with, the attitude or vibe your employees give off. Delta is a great example of that. Your experience with their culture starts with their employees as soon as you check in. Leadership is not a title or name, it's an action and example of how you treat people. It is how you lead your family, relationships, business or organization, and most importantly—your life. As a leader, character and integrity toward others is important, and whether you benefit from them or not, it's part of who you are.

"TRUE LEADERS DO NOT CREATE MORE FOLLOWERS; THEY CREATE MORE LEADERS."

VEHICLES

I spoke about this earlier regarding the question I was asked on where I was on a scale from 1–10 in my life in time and money. I said -2, and there were three things I had to change to get to 10: mentor, educate, and vehicle. If someone said they would either give you a Lamborghini or a tug boat, which one would you take? Most people would say the Lamborghini, but it really depends on what you need it for. I call that "hood rich" where you buy things you can't afford to impress people you don't even like or know.

I bought a "Rolex" from China when I was 19. It came in a really nice package, and I thought I was getting a great deal for only $79.99. I was going to be so cool! Until about three months later when it started to turn green and the "diamonds" were falling out. That was when I realized why you buy the real thing. It's okay to want nice things, but in moderation and acting our wage. I call it deferred consumption or delayed gratification. Choosing the tugboat is actually the better choice because you can make money with it, travel across the water, and move things with it to make income. It is an asset, not a liability. Sure, it may not be as pretty as a Lamborghini, but it will eventually allow you to purchase a nice car if you choose but still have cash flow coming in.

Choosing your vehicle in life will give you the outcome you want to increase your life resume, which is the total of events you experience with those you enjoy being around throughout your life. Although you may like your career or business, are the outcomes everything you wanted? Look at people that invent something, say a new type of mop. They don't necessarily love mops, but they love the outcome of how it created wealth for them and their family. You'll meet people that say they love what they do. That's great if they truly do.

But would you do the same thing you're doing now if you had to do it for free? That's an honest question you must ask yourself. We like going to the gym because we like the results we get from it. If we never got results, would we still go to the gym?

How about going to bars and drinking a beer that costs $1 but they charge you $7, and you are drinking too many carbs with people you don't know and can barely have a conversation with because it's too loud. You talk with your eyes and pray you can read lips. In the end, there's no great result, and you're not even sure why you went.

I'd rather go to a nice lounge or bar with the right people and a good atmosphere where we talk about each other and business and the future and I can write-off the meal because it's a business meal. My night out is now an asset, not a liability.

Find the vehicle in your life that will fulfill you but also give you the outcome you desire. I chose the ecommerce world because I was a broke college student wanting to build something in my dorm room. Ten years later, I'm still blessed to live off of what I built. Yes, you will have adjustments along the way and "life" will happen, but it's nice to know you are making asset decisions every day.

I break down life into three vehicles:

Jobs – Trading your time for money helping someone else achieve their dream

Careers – Doctor, accountant, lawyer, engineer, actor, dancer, athlete, host, etc.

Entrepreneur – Designer, ecommerce sites, real estate, independent singer, services, business owners, inventors

Choose what will make you fulfilled but also allow you to impact society. Ecommerce allows me the freedom to work wherever I want, and I am able to be a mentor to others and create charities to positively impact the world. Pick the vehicle you want in your life that will truly make you happy and create the results you always desired.

STORY TELLING AND BRAND

People buy into stories and a person before they buy into an organization. Your brand and story have to be organic and natural. People don't want to be sold anything; they want a story that shows how you can help them. In the movie *Rocky*, we loved the story that Sylvester Stallone created because we related to him so much. The theme song and story connected with the audience, which is why everyone loves it. Stallone did not try to be someone he wasn't. Instead, he was real which is why people bought into him and the story.

When you try to be someone you're not, your story feels processed and not real. People know from the feel of it that it is manufactured. Look at Coca-Cola and their branding, and you will notice they have done a few things well with their story-telling. For example, they use Santa in commercials and advertisements during the holidays. During the summer, they play up the refreshing cold bottle and also print names on each bottle so people can share a bottle with a friend who has the same name.

Branding techniques and storytelling are important to the income stream you choose. People buy into the vision and mission of the company, not the product. People love working for Apple and Google because of their story. First, you need to:

1. Identify your story

2. Define the product/service behind that story

3. Discover who will buy into that story and benefit from your product/service

Brands die when the story dies or stops being told the proper way. Learn to own your story and live it. Make it who you are so you don't need to change your mask in different situations. You are an original, not a carbon copy. If you're not being authentic yet, this will be the most liberating feeling in the world. Your story lasts for a long time and will continue to be told like a tree planted now will produce shade for years to come.

"KEEP CREATING THESE NEW STORIES IN LIFE. LEARN TO EMPTY THE BACKPACK OF YOUR PAST SO THAT YOUR FUTURE JOURNEY IS LIGHTER AND BRIGHTER."

WORK

You must have a strong work ethic. When I look back at my career in baseball, especially in college, we worked six to seven days a week and put a winning team on the field that no one could compete against. Our practice consisted of maybe one day off, four days a week working out, and two to three days doing agility workouts, which are running and explosive movements. Our bodies were always being worked and never rested. The funniest was when our legs were so sore that we walked around campus like ducks. I remember driving to class because my legs just didn't work. We always worked hard to make sure we gave our best out on the field.

My junior year is when I started my business, and I was going to school as a double major, playing baseball, doing workouts, doing homework, working a little with baseball lessons, and building my business on the side from 7:00 to 11:00 every night. I then did homework after that till around 2:00 a.m.

and woke up at 7:00 a.m. to start the day over. I was operating on 4 to 6 hours of sleep and taking naps wherever I could. Some of you may have a family and have a lot going on, and that's why the health and organization rocks will help you to focus and use your time wisely. Especially with my schedule, I needed to be decently organized to operate all those things at only 20 years old. I had meetings to attend and clients to sit down with, but I also had to balance my personal life as well. You don't need to be a robot, but you do need to work. When I saw my roommates and friends wasting their time, I realized I was doing something different to build my future.

You can't have a million-dollar dream with a minimum-wage work ethic. To this day, I know I can work harder and more efficiently than most people I know. Hard work doesn't accomplish as much as efficient work does. In baseball, you can take 300 bad swings or take 50 great swings that create a great outcome. Ted Williams and Warren Buffet had something in common; they both knew what pitch to swing at. They knew their strike zone and what area of the strike zone that made them hit the best. Ted Williams created a system (and wrote a book about it) for him to know his average depending on where the baseball was thrown. He knew where he should and shouldn't swing. If we only got 20 swings in life, we would be careful about what we swung at and be more strategic. If you know your zone and what you're good at, you will increase your probability of succeeding.

There is something called an "immigrant work ethic," and when you look at people who were not born in this country, they have an extra drive. They come to America to achieve more and prosper because back at the home they left, their life was capped out. They locked the door behind them and have no choice but to go forward—to succeed. You will notice they have a different energy and appreciation of life; they're bigger dreamers, and they get things done.

I'm not saying that if you were born here, you need to move to another country, live there for a while, and then come back to have this same work ethic. It's something you can study. You even see it in sports with people who come from a hard childhood or grew up in a difficult area. They have more pep in their step. They fight harder to create a great life for their family. They are consistent every day and do not give up no matter what. I remember when I was 23 years old, I left my house just because I needed that extra push. At 24, I moved into my first home and felt what it was like to pay big bills. That push sometimes lights a fire in you to go out and crush it.

While in Vermont I was in the passenger seat looking at the beautiful streams of water and snow as my brother was driving. I saw those streams as resembling life. All winter, there was snow and ice on top, but under that ice, the water was still flowing. As the weather became warmer, the water and its power started to push the ice away. Even though water is soft, its strength is in its consistent movement. You sometimes need to be patient as the seasons of life change so you can showcase your true strength, just like that stream. At times, the obstacles of ice may feel unbreakable, but have faith a new season is coming that will allow you to remove that ice with efficient and consistent work. Your season will arrive.

ATTITUDE

Your attitude controls your altitude in your income, in your dreams, and in the people around you. I speak about this a lot when I talk about the rocks of personal and spiritual growth, but as someone who has goals to achieve, you must remain cool, calm, and collected through adversity. As I write this book, I'm going through some challenges personally and in business, and I've chosen to apply these principles to my own life. You can't tell someone to have a great attitude if you are always down. You should try to even have a great attitude toward HATERS. HATERS stands for Having Anger Toward Everyone Reaching Success. Be thankful for people who support you and those who maybe don't. My best friend once said to me,

> *"Steven, if you want to make everyone happy, go sell ice cream!"*
>
> —*Bryan Lewis*

People that are "crushing" it in life to make a difference in this world, don't have time to gossip. They are too busy making a difference and a mark in society. Learn to stay in your lane along this journey and some will join the ride while other's will continue to complain about the ride. I had a friend recently send me this quote "The same people that brought you pain check your page to see if you're happy." We try to impress everyone in every way, but at the end of the day, you can't please everyone, and you need to make *you* happy. Your attitude is like a price tag; it shows how valuable you are without approval from everything and everyone.

> "YOUR MIND OR SPIRIT IN LIFE IS EITHER LIKE AN OCEAN OR A POND; IT WILL BE EITHER ROUGH OR CALM. YOU CHOOSE."

DREAMS

Michael Jordan said, "Some people want it to happen; some people wish for it to happen; some people make it happen."

My dreams have always been what has pushed me, even to this day. I don't know where everything will go with this project, including the book, website, podcast, Project Impact Charities, and Seven Rock Life brand, but I pray that it leaves an impact for society to help people live better lives. I am excited that 50% of every book sold and every item purchased on SevenRockLife.com will be donated and will go back to those less fortunate. If God gives you abundance, don't keep it just for yourselves. Are you able to get some of those dream things you wanted? Of course, get some of those things out of the way, just don't let them own your desire or purpose. Growing up, I remember my dad frequently saying that if you like something in life, work hard, make more money, and go buy it.

I think dreams are like the fuel to your car. Many of us have a car ready to go, but the fuel tank is either empty or has the wrong fuel. But when you carry the right fuel, you become a vehicle that goes.

Maybe that fuel is to impact others' lives, or your family, wife, kids, cars, boats, etc. But something has to fuel you to get you going. I have discovered that people who lack energy and enthusiasm lack dreams.

It has taken me 31 years of life experiences with highs and lows to get to this point of creating this book. It only took me a couple of months to write it, but I needed that fuel to get going. Who knew my lowest point in life would be the perfect time to write it. The biggest obstacle you may have with your dreams is you need to make sure your dreams are big enough so you can include others in it! Find something that gives you passion every day because you never want to "work full-time and live a part-time life."

"IF YOUR DREAM CAN'T FIT ANYONE ELSE, THEN IT'S SMALL. IT'S A SELFISH DREAM, AND YOU WILL BE LONELY."

Remember that everything in this world, before it came about, was thought about in someone's mind or dreams and then executed. They say the #1 thing that people bring to the grave is all the wishes and dreams that never came true, all the times you didn't say *I love you* or *I am sorry* because of anger. Don't live a life of regrets. Don't ever feel you're too old or not worthy to accomplish something. Your belief and dreams are so important. Steve Harvey was 38 years old when he got his break for TV, Sylvester Stallone was 30 when *Rocky* was released, Colonel Sanders of KFC was 65 years old when he finally "made it," and Abraham Lincoln become president at 51 years old, after being one of the most defeated men in the world. Sometimes, you need an event or something to happen to force you to go out and purchase the dreams you always wanted. Sometimes our first dreams of life are just a draft, getting us ready for the real thing.

"THE BIGGEST ADVENTURE YOU CAN TAKE IS TO LIVE THE LIFE OF YOUR DREAMS."
—OPRAH

I wrote this poem at 15 years old, and my amazing sister put it on paper in my weight room growing up where I looked at it every day.

Dream Big and Dream Often

Some don't
Some can't
Some do
Some can
What matters is if you try
To be what you can be
To do what you can do
To be who you are
It's you who makes the decision
To be who you are
Or to do what you want
No one is in charge
Of what you are
And what you want!

by Steven Mazzurco (age 15)

Quiz

Rate this Rock for yourself on a scale from 1–10.

_____

_____

What was your top take-away from this chapter?

_____

_____

What gaps do you have in this Rock?

_____

_____

What is your game plan and action to fix these gaps?

_____

_____

6

ORGANIZATION

Many people today suffer from anxiety; I say it's more of a "clutter issue." Let me explain. Too often we get overwhelmed with too many things. When all of your thoughts are in your mind and not organized on paper in front of you, you feel cluttered and overwhelmed. Personal organization is one of the biggest influences on your success and happiness. Your personal organization skills and systems help you feel more fulfilled, productive, and achieve a mental state of overall well-being. What's easier to go through; woods with many trees and a lot of bushes or one that has been cleared?

Did you grow up in a house where the garage was a mess, and when you needed a tool, it couldn't be found? If you use something, put it back in the same spot. When the grass grows high in a field, it becomes hard to walk on and can't see the dog running in it. You need to maintain it and keep it short or bugs start to come around.

Planning for the future is important, but planning for the present is happening today. We sometimes plan so much for the future that we forget the present. When you drive a car, you enter your destination in the GPS, which tracks where you are going and how to get there most efficiently. Well, this is the same thing with organization and setting goals and promises. These steps are key to getting you on track.

"WHAT YOU WANT IN LIFE CANNOT BE A GOAL, IT MUST BE A PROMISE TO YOURSELF, YOUR FAMILY, AND SOCIETY."

Here are four places to clear the clutter in your life and keep you focused on what is important.

TO-DO LIST

There are different types of to-do lists, and you can have to-do lists for home, life, and work. I like to have these to-do lists on my phone and also on my desk on paper. I put a palm tree emoji next to very important things on my phone list (palm trees remind me of warm weather, especially living up north.) Also, make sure your desk doesn't have papers everywhere, or things will get lost. Use only 1–2 papers for your to-do list because it keeps your desk clear and doesn't overwhelm you. It becomes like a game to check each item off, and it feels very rewarding.

I was at a conference, and the gentleman who was speaking was talking about his sales team and the to-do list they use. When it's time to send something out, he says, "Hit the list!" Make your to-do list fun and productive. I like having a list of 15 or fewer with the top items being the most important. They should be on one piece of paper so you don't get overwhelmed. If you have too many lists, papers, or reminders on your phone, you'll go crazy.

Here are three areas to add to your list.

Home stuff can be organizing your closet, garage, or anywhere. Many will say this is a waste of time, but the reality is we waste time looking for things when we're not organized. It clears your thinking when you put things in the right places. One big help is to clear and throw out or donate things you truly don't need. Many people become hoarders and still have things like textbooks from middle school or their first baby blanket. Also, when you have people over, it shows you are an organized person. The state of your house leaves a strong first impression on people.

Life stuff gets a little tricky because it depends on how consuming your work is. I break down life things into the top 10 to 15 things to do with the top item being the most important. With anything more than 15, you get overwhelmed. Most likely, anything you list after 15 is not serious or does not need to be done right away. Items on your life to-do list might include a doctor appointment, fixing house stuff, kids' events, vehicle registration, oil change, pay bills, gift for the spouse, etc.

Work things are projects or meetings you need to do to grow in whatever your business or career goals are. Write those things down. This area basically grows your income if you do work effectively in this area. Often, home or life things may make us feel good and accomplished, but they don't progress our income. We sometimes get stuck in those other two categories.

NOTES/IDEAS

This is a fun section, especially if you are growing personally or are creative. You should have a separate section in your phone/notebook for ideas you hear or think of. While writing this book, I would write down ideas or things I heard that would fit well in a certain section. I used my phone because I'm on the go a lot and would email the notes to myself as a backup. Writing things down is content that allows you to learn and process things.

Anytime you hear something that hits home, write it down so you can embrace it and feel good about it. Make sure you keep this in one place because if you have too many areas of notes or ideas, it confuses you. The best example is like a food court when there are so many good choices you don't know which one to pick, and you waste time thinking which one would be best. Notes are things that will help you become a better person, more efficient in business, and will improve your life. Ideas are things that will allow you to be creative, such as rebranding your website, social media profiles, date night idea for your spouse, etc.

"HOW DO YOU ORGANIZE A SPACE PARTY?
YOU PLANET."

CALENDAR

Mini-whiteboard or regular notebook calendars and phone calendars are great for scheduling. The whiteboards you can't take around with you, obviously, so your book or phone calendars are necessary. Take time during the week to organize. Calendars allow you to make your time more effective. If you go through life without adding to your "life/work calendar" your daily actions will control your outcome and potentially get you off-course from the promises you made. I see many people waste time at the gym and they are there for two to three hours, but only spend 45 minutes working out. The rest of the time, they are socializing or on their phone. I leverage my time effectively as often as possible. And it's not just work time. For example, this week I spent three hours with my parents for breakfast, and we drove around the area and by the water. But that was intentional time I spent with them. Quality time is better than quantity.

You can spend six hours with them, but if you're on your phone, then you're not really there. After I was done visiting my parents, I had meetings and work to do from 2:00 p.m. until 11:00 p.m., and I did not check my phone once when I was with them. Later this week, I'm hanging out with my little niece and her mom for three hours. That's me and her time, so I won't be doing anything else. I even blocked it out in my schedule. Another reason why I built my ecommerce business is that I wanted to buy back days and hours during the week so I can spend time with the people I love or do things to progress in life.

If you have a spouse, you can link your calendars so you are on the same page and things don't overlap. Learning to leverage your time and calendar is key to growing in life. We all have 24 hours a day. Many people have fillers like TV or social media, and it crushes the productive nature of whatever they are trying to accomplish. I love how the iPhone tells you how much time you spent on apps; it shows you how much time you truly waste. The past three months while working on projects and not being distracted, I was able to write a book, develop two websites, create vlog/blog interviews, start a podcast, start a clothing brand, grow my other business, be a life/business coach, and start the process to team with organizations for Project Impact Charities. At times, it is best to allow someone else to look over your schedule and see what gaps you can fix to help you make the most of your days and weeks. Sometimes we don't see the gaps in our scheduling and being efficient, but someone who is successful will. I have realized from experience that when you schedule things like time with family, meetings, gym, catching up with friends, that you put yourself in a situation that you can't do anything else. It locks in whatever you committed to so nothing else distracts you and takes you away from what you booked. Plan to succeed and grow, or plan to fail—it's your choice.

"BOOK YOUR CALENDAR OR YOUR CALENDAR
WILL BOOK YOUR LIFE."

CLEAN HOUSE/APARTMENT/CAR

When you clean these, you clean your life. I remember one time I was about to get into a car of someone's and I saw half-empty bags of fast food that had been in there for weeks. I looked inside and said I'd walk. What's interesting is the person's car was a direct correlation to that person's life: a mess and confused about many things.

At times, it may make sense to hire cleaning people to help out if it's in your budget. It will be time you can spend building your business, being with family or kids, or doing other things you enjoy. If that's not an option, take time throughout the week to maintain your home and just make sure to put things away right away. It builds up out of nowhere, and then your place is a mess, and you ask yourself how things got that way. I'll tell you why—you didn't put things away! We have tickets for violations with vehicles; we should have tickets for people who let their home become a mess. Some things are close to a felony, like never cleaning your dishes or leaving food out so your house smells. Clear the clutter, and you will feel better about your life.

"MY LIFE IS JUST ABOUT AS ORGANIZED AS THE
$5 BIN IN WALMART."

Also, take care of your yard and garden. My brother and I came up with a theory, and it's pretty accurate from our research. People's lawns reflect their lives. If they take care of their yard, they usually do the same with their life. We knew someone who was doing well and then their lawn started to go downhill. Lo and behold, their life started to go downhill a few months later. They were having trouble with their business, and it showed in other areas of their life. This is not always true, but our observation shows it's usually accurate. When people come to visit you, the first thing they see is if your cars and house are clean. It creates an inviting environment, a special place for you and your family. Also, always make sure your environment is dust free because it can create allergies and bacteria can form when not taking care properly. Respect your surroundings, and they will respect you.

"WE SOMETIMES USE NATURE LIKE A CREDIT CARD WITH NO LIMIT."

I recently learned that your wardrobe can actually restrict your thinking. When you have too many choices or too many old clothes, it overwhelms you, and you lose time trying to pick the perfect outfit. Many successful people stick to two or three colors so it's simple, which allows them not to waste tons of hours over a lifetime. You can even hire someone at a low cost to organize your wardrobe and give you styles to wear with what you already own. Mentorship in dressing is something I never knew about. I've worn some funky things before. I'm still not there or as cool and hip as I could be, but I'm working on getting better. I've learned that if you stick with white, black, and gray, you'll be cool.

ORGANIZATION

When organizing your home, have one spot where you put your keys, shoes, coat, etc. so you don't waste time looking for them.

Here are ten points to remember:

1. Write things down

2. Make schedules and have deadlines

3. Don't procrastinate

4. Give everything a home

5. Declutter regularly

6. Keep only what you need

7. Know when to discard items

8. Look for great deals or bargains

9. Delegate responsibilities

10. Get organized

"LEAVE EVERYTHING AND EVERY SITUATION BETTER THEN YOU FOUND IT."

We sometimes don't respect, not only our own stuff, but also our surroundings. It never made sense to me, I see people throw things outside their car window. They may think that it's okay because they don't live there, but the truth is that all of us live everywhere. Our home is the entire world, and we must take care of it. If you rent a home, treat it with respect. If you stay at a friend's house, take care of the dishes or the room you stayed in. Offer to clean or take the trash out. How you do one thing is how you do everything.

"MY TWO FAVORITE WAYS TO SAVE TIME ARE HOT POCKETS AND UNCRUSTABLES SANDWICHES."

SCHEDULING AND TIME

Scheduling is important for making every day count. We all have the same 24 hours in every day, and when people say they're too busy, it tells me they never audit what they are actually busy doing. The time you spend will be either an asset or a liability. For me, my asset time is time I spend asking myself if I focused on the Seven Rocks and did I progress in all seven that day. If I didn't, I ask why and then reorganize my schedule. Let's look at an example from today's schedule:

- Gym (Health)

- New friendship (Relationship)

- Spiritual leadership call (Spiritual)

- Paid bills (Finance)

- Had two meetings and three phone calls (Income Stream)

- Cleaned house/added to calendar (Organization)

- Read this morning/audio (Personal Growth)

So, by 6:27 p.m., I completed all seven rocks. Now, you may think you can't accomplish work in all seven areas because you have too much work. I call that TOB or Transfer of Blame. Winners find a way period. Whether you have kids or a job, you need to organize better and learn how to outsource more. I built my ecommerce business when I was in college playing Division I baseball, working on a double major, and working baseball lessons.

"STOP TRYING TO BE PERFECT AND START BEING PERFECT WITH YOUR EXECUTION."

How did I use my time wisely? I woke up early for class, listened to audios on the way, and built relationships with new people, I then went to workouts for baseball, and then went to work on my business, I would come home late and do homework until 1:00 or 2:00 in the morning. Two to three times a month, I would visit my parents who were about 30 minutes away. I spent quality time with friends and family, and I also spent time networking and building my business relationships.

You can always figure out a way if your dreams are big enough. If you had an hourglass with sand representing how much time you had left, I think you would spend your time a lot more efficiently. How you choose to do that is completely up to you. You can do a year's worth of work in three months if you focus.

You must learn to turn off the noise around you whether it be friends, family, or just distractions. It's okay to put your phone on airplane mode besides on the plane while you are doing things. The phone is a great device but can also be distracting and consuming. Successful people trying to accomplish things, are not always available. They are what I call "productively busy" and will not always be there because they are making an impact in this world. Don't be too available and learn to say no. It may be hard, but I wasn't able to make every family event. At first, they didn't understand it, but now they see the life it can produce. It took time in succeeding to change their perspective.

"PEOPLE PLAN AND PREPARE MORE FOR A VACATION THEN THEY DO FOR THEIR LIVES."

OUTSOURCING AND TECH

In today's world, our tech life has truly made things more efficient. Like I explained earlier, you need to use tech to make asset decisions, not liability decisions. Time is the biggest currency of life, so you need to know how you can buy it back. Some ways to buy back your time include:

- Ordering food on an app or using meal prep companies

- Hire cleaning people

- Hire lawn maintenance companies

- Outsource your company projects

- Use reminders on your phone

- Using your computer to write a book, educate yourself, or do work on

- Track your diet to be healthy

- Hire a nanny

- Use mobile banking

- Book flights online

- Listen to podcasts or audiobooks to gain knowledge while in your car

You get the point of how to buy back time or make your life more efficient. Learning to outsource things that you're not good at or what takes up time you could spend creating more income. This is all part of organization. I order things on Amazon, and it saves me many hours of shopping. I even have my household items, toiletries, and health products delivered every month to my door. I love it, it's like Christmas every month.

As I'm writing this book today, the cleaning people spent three hours cleaning the house as I did a workout at the gym, built a new relationship, met some new people, did a video call with my spiritual counselor, and drove back home while listening to a podcast and taking a phone call. If you have a 9–5 schedule for work, then your hours before and after that are key to your success. Maybe you have breaks in between, and you're able to work on things then as well. Winners find a way and don't come home and relax; they crush it to live that thriving life.

Will there be times you need to shut off and enjoy yourself? Of course. That could be a hobby, movie, or time with friends or family. Just make sure to work on that balance and not let "hanging out" take over your time. I realized in today's world that: The new entertainment is educating yourself to be better and making an impact in society.

We often try to consume too many things in life and don't know how to delegate. Companies that have this issue can't grow. But even on a personal level, you need to learn how to delegate to thrive. Yes, there are things you may enjoy doing. For example, I like mowing my own lawn. It's relaxing for me making those straight lines. Some people don't feel that way. Of course, it only takes me 30 minutes to mow my lawn. If it took three hours, I would hire someone in a heartbeat. This is based on your budget, but if you do income-producing activities during that time, you will earn it back.

"YOUR BRAIN IS LIKE AN EMPTY HOUSE THAT ALLOWS YOU TO DESIGN YOUR LIFE THE WAY YOU WANT. BUT IF ITS ALREADY FURNISHED AND CLUTTERED, IT'S HARD TO IMAGINE WHAT IT CAN BE."

FILLERS

Clearing the clutter in your life is key to your success. I believe the biggest distractions today are television (including online video such as Netflix, Amazon Prime, and YouTube), social media, and gossip. I challenge you to get rid of all of these for two weeks and fill that extra time with reading more, listening to positive or educational audios, building better offline relationships, and working on the Seven Rocks of Life. I guarantee you will feel better. Fillers are what make you think you are productive, but you're productive for someone else's dream, not your own goals and dreams. If someone is racing and constantly looks at their opponent, they will probably lose because they are so worried about their competition.

Learn to stay in your lane. The fillers in your life can even be family and friends. Yes, they are very important, but you need to control your time. I have said this before, but even as I write this part of the book, my phone is in airplane mode so I don't have distractions. Many little things you incorporate in your life allow your mind to be extremely efficient. Do you ever see a pro athlete on his phone during a game?

"BUILD YOURSELF A LIFESTYLE OR WATCH OTHERS
ENJOY THEIR LIFESTYLE."

You may not be a pro athlete competing in a game but every day you're competing to give your family and others a better life. Stop letting fillers own you. During the summer, you could spend a lot of time at the beach, but at the end of the day, do you want to be at a local beach or traveling to beaches around the world? It's all about choices. Filler time is a temporary fill that eventually becomes empty. You need to look at those gaps in your schedule and ask how you can fill this gap with actions that produce asset outcomes, not liability outcomes.

In wrapping up this chapter about the rock of organization and clearing clutter out of your life, it's important to understand that it is about what you do in preparation that allows you to be efficient. With a certain project or goal, preparing for it is key so that when it's all done, it's not all mixed up being put together wrong. If you try to put together a puzzle with no blueprint, it comes out wrong or takes more time. I'll share a secret—I have a suitcase explosion problem. I was on a trip with my brother not too long ago, and I asked if he wanted to put his stuff by me. He said no way because my suitcase always blows up. I didn't believe him, but that night he was proven right when my suitcase blew up everywhere. That is an area of organization I'm still working on today. Even when I go away, I have a habit of keeping too much stuff in my suitcase.

It's a never-ending process to get your life organized. See what gaps you can improve. Don't try to be perfect because you will go crazy, but instead learn how to have a balance so that you feel good about your life. Take the time to put things in order and have a correct game plan.

While working on all of my projects, which took about 90 days to create my website, writing a book, podcast, clothing brand, charity, mentoring people in business life and living my seven rocks of life I had two great friends ask how I do it all. I answered as follows:

ORGANIZATION

- When others are sleeping, you're awake

- When others are complaining, you're solving issues

- When others are watching television, you're watching your projects grow

- When others are talking about celebrities, you're talking about the people your helping,

- When others talk about what they did in the past, you're talking about what you're doing in the future,

- When others are listening to music, you're listening to podcasts to learn

- When others are reading magazines, you're reading books that make your mind sharper

- When others are self-consumed with themselves, your giving to others who need help

- When others complain about the weather, you thank the universe for life and water

- When others are asking friends and parents for advice, you're asking God or a great mentor what's next

QUIZ

Rate this Rock for yourself on a scale from 1–10.

_____

_____

What was your top take-away from this chapter?

_____

_____

What gaps do you have in this Rock?

_____

_____

What is your game plan and action to fix these gaps?

_____

_____

7

PERSONAL GROWTH

When I first heard about personal growth, I wondered why I never learned about this in school! I realized that personal growth is like the interior of a home. If the outside looks good, but there's no furniture inside, it will be very empty. The inside of our hearts, spirit, and mind need attention to grow and progress. We are either surviving or thriving. I think being curious to learn is key to true progress. Being curious about people and life is fascinating. Knowing a little bit about a lot of things helps you to have great conversations.

When you're mentally stimulated and not distracted, you start to gain perspective of yourself. I think we let too many distractions keep us from discovering our true selves. We then try to live our life and walk around with a mask that is not truly us, just as in the movie, *The Mask*, with Jim Carrey. (The only part that scared me in that movie was when that little dog put the green mask on. I still have nightmares about that.)

Have you ever felt like you had a governor in life, something that restricts your speed like they use on go-karts to slow them down so people who act irresponsibly don't go out of control? The same thing happens in your life because you are not becoming your true identity. I recommend creating an identity document. This is a letter written by you that makes you realize what your true mission is in life. It also gives you a code of conduct of how you want to operate, what your character and values are, and what you stand for.

THE PORTRAIT OF YOUR LIFE

The four things we want:

- Acceptance

- Identity

- Security

- Purpose

We want to be accepted, but we need to accept ourselves first. We must not live in others' lives because this becomes a dangerous spot to be. I know for me there has been a time of comparison that has truly hurt me. We compare lives, looks, bodies, cars, and relationships, and it affects our self-identity. You look to social media, like so many are doing, which then hurts your personal self-worth.

You must be able to love yourself right now for a breakthrough about to happen. It's like the seasons.

You need to enjoy winter when you're in it because, after that, spring and summer come. And then people start complaining it's too hot during summer and want fall but then they get mad the cold is coming when just a few months before they were complaining about how hot it was. You know you've done that, and so have I.

When you think about the word "identity," it's becoming something and sometimes figuring out who you truly are and what you are all about. Maybe you remember as a kid when every few weeks you or maybe your friends in middle or high school would dress in different styles like punk, preppy, thug, or jock. You weren't sure which identity would help you fit into society. Your identity is your true prized possession. Remember, a dog does not try to act like a cat because they know its true identity. Sometimes, we let society choose our identity instead of allowing God to help us find it. At times in your life, you may have to go shopping for your identity this way you can have a stocked fridge inside you so others will feel full around you because you truly feel full about yourself.

"YOUR IDENTITY IS LIKE YOUR PASSPORT. IF YOU LOSE IT, YOU'LL BE STUCK IN THE SAME PLACE."

Be anchored in your identity. I remember over the summer I was with my best friend in California with two other friends, and we were on a boat we rented. We decided to watch the air show by Huntington Beach, and it was amazing! The one issue we had before we got settled in was that there were over 1,000 boats there, so moving around was tough, but we found a spot to stay in and were thankful it was a calm day.

When we got to our spot, the anchor button on the boat wouldn't work. We ended up having to manually put the anchor and chain down 60 feet. When we finished, we thought we were all set, but then our boat started to drift away from our original spot just as we were ready to eat and enjoy the show. We started to drift toward other boats with the anchor dragging. The girls were laughing and concerned at the same time as we started to figure things out. We had to pick the anchor back up, get the boat back in place and try again for it to catch. After trying five times, we finally got the anchor to stay in the proper spot and grab the ocean floor properly. The undercurrent was strong and moving the anchor too much for us to stay in one spot.

Along this journey of life, we have currents that sometimes shift our identity because we're not anchored in who we truly are. We sometimes need to lift up the anchor and place it in the right area for it to lock in the way it needs to. When you're properly rooted in life with who you are, where you're going, and who is around you, your boat will be solid and not move or shift with the storms of life.

"LEARN TO BE THE CONDUCTOR OF YOUR LIFE.
TO OFTEN WE LET OTHERS DO THE DRIVING
INSTEAD OF US PAINTING THE PORTRAIT OF LIFE
WE ALWAYS WANTED!

MOAT

A moat is a deep, wide ditch surrounding a castle, fort, or town, typically filled with water and intended as a defense against attack. How does this relate to personal growth? You need to figure out what your moat is that protects you from outside forces that may try to take your peace, happiness or identity. The castle is you, and your personal growth is the moat that protects you from these external problems. Sometimes, you need to be attacked or have something happen that shakes you to gain the moat you truly need. The castle that is your mind and soul is key to your fulfilled life of true joy. Work on that protection every day, too, and it will be the thing that makes you stand out compared to everyone else around you. Here is something I realized recently that we all have two bodies in life: our physical body and our emotional body. The challenge is we let our emotional body be connected to our physical body, which is why people at times numb their pain with drugs or alcohol. Our physical body is not hurting, it is our emotional body that is giving us pain. If you learn to separate both, you will build a moat that sets you apart from everyone else. You will not allow the pressures of life to affect your beautiful castle you have worked so hard to build.

SO HOW DO YOU GO ABOUT PERSONAL GROWTH?

The main activity is to read books every day that inspire you in different areas of life, whether it is in relationship, business, spiritual, or mental toughness, you need to fertilize your mind with constant good thinking. We pollute our brains with bad shows, news, or things we read, and it hurts our environment.

The next thing I recommend is to listen to great audios or podcasts that inspire you or provide valuable knowledge. I remember hearing a story about two men who went to cut wood. Both had used axes before. One guy said he was going to the store to get a sharpener, the other said that it was a waste of time. The guy who bought the sharpener came back and found the other guy wasn't even halfway done. The guy with who kept his ax sharp was done an hour before the other guy, even though he left to go to the store. He went inside, got warm, and had a drink. Sharpen your mind and personal growth with wisdom, and you will live a life that is more efficient and helps you get through it more easily.

The thing you can do for personal growth is to attend events or visit people who are ahead of you in life. Sometimes we are afraid of change, but in the end, you need to change your ZIP code to move forward. Have you ever worked out with someone who was stronger than you and you go to pull or pick up the weight and just look at them and say, Dude, why so much weight?" That's your sign that you need to work harder.

ENVIRONMENT

Invest time and money going to seminars or networking opportunities to be around the best players. As children, we invest in sports leagues and lessons, but when we get older, we forget to invest in what helps us do better in the sport of life. Remember the investing mentality vs. the spending mentality. These three things are key to helping you grow, and there are many organizations and content out there for you to update your mind software with the correct info. We too often try to operate on software that hasn't been updated in years.

You will notice that the best conversations are not surface level conversations; they are conversations that make you feel good, have purpose, and are not about the same old things. I'm truly careful with who and what is put into my mind. You work so hard to make it strong, so you want to keep it on track. Why would you let someone destroy your perfect lawn on which you worked so hard? I have seen people grow personally but eventually go downhill all because of association. When you hang out with people who make you uncomfortable in a good way, it is because they push you to become better.

"HOW YOU TREAT OTHERS IS A DIRECT REFLECTION OF HOW YOU TREAT YOURSELF."

Self-love, in a humbling way, is very important. The vibe you give off in life will affect the tribe around you. For me, at certain times of my life, I really didn't like who I was becoming. It showed in how I treated people; I was always short-tempered. Having grace and empathy toward others is important, but when you don't truly love who you are, where you're going, and the people you're doing it with, life becomes empty.

SELF-TALK

The language you use when talking about yourself or others is also very important. When I was playing baseball, if I did not speak positive affirmations, my game was much worse. I saw players with great talent who did poorly because of their attitude and self-talk, saying things like, "I suck, I'm no good, I can never get a break," etc. These things we speak out into the universe are powerful and can either hurt or help us and everyone around us.

Look up "Dr. Emoto's water experiment," and you will see how powerful words can even change water and how it looks. It is really remarkable. Our bodies consist of 60% water, so the words we choose can have a powerful effect on us. Life or death is in the power of the tongue. Be careful with what is said about yourself and learn to practice exercises that teach self-talk. You may feel weird at first, but many athletes and successful people do it. Try every day for seven days straight to wake up and speak only positive things for five minutes, and you will see a difference in how you feel and your attitude.

SIX HUMAN NEEDS

Anthony Robbins talks about six human needs we all desire:

1. Certainty

2. Uncertainty/Variety

3. Significance

4. Love and Connection

5. Growth

6. Contribution

Let's talk about **Certainty** first. In life we do like to know that we can control some things, whether it be our car starting in the morning, getting paid on Friday, knowing your dog will love you no matter what, having hot water at home, or food in the fridge. Most of the time, we don't like variety; we want consistency. We wouldn't be very happy if every day we woke up it was a flip of the coin as to whether or not our car would start.

Uncertainty can be like a sports game where, if you know who's going to win, it's boring. Other things could be a surprise your family or friends do for you, like a party. We like that and enjoy that uncertainty at times, especially because we feel loved. We might even enjoy wondering how people will react to a project we've been working on because we worked hard and enjoy a positive response for our accomplishments.

Significance is something all humans want. Remember, the two days you die are the day you pass away and the day your name is never said again because you never made a difference in this world. We enjoy making an impact, whether it's for society, family, friends, or just the world in general. Akon is a great example of this where he took his fame and money as a singer and used it to build a solar grid in Africa to supply electricity for those who did not have it. We love that type of significance.

Even if you have the chance to help some in need on the side of the road, we will sometimes go out of our way to help another person more than ourselves. Heroes are remembered, like on 9/11, because they made such an impact in serving and helping others. You were proud to be a responder who worked that day. That's how we operate, and it makes us feel good. Project Impact and other charities are about impacting lives and saving them and raises money to help those who need it to feed people or build schools.

Love and connection are like heat during the winter. It makes us warm. Who's happier to see you when you get home, your spouse or your dog? The reason we love pets is that they love us unconditionally, even when we smell bad. It doesn't work that way between humans, unfortunately. When we develop strong bonds with friends or family, we connect like a chain, not just a rope. We strive for those genuine connections as humans.

"THE CONCERT OF LIFE IS NOT THE SAME
WHEN IT IS BY YOURSELF."
—VINNY MAZZURCO

We enjoy **growth** because we love progress as humans. Progressing is what makes us happy. Achieving keeps us going, and when we stop making progress, we get down. For me, growing in all seven rocks of life helps me feel fulfilled. It's not always easy, but it's something I strive for.

Contribution is about giving back and being able to help others live better. It's not what you give to people; it's what you leave in people that matters. This includes going out of your way to help a friend or helping with a charity. Contribution creates results or helps something to advance.

"LOVE AND CONNECTION ARE LIKE THE OCEAN AND THE SHORE MEETING. THE LOVE IS THE OCEAN, AND THE LAND IS THE CONNECTION, AND TOGETHER THEY BLEND."

CONTROLLING YOUR RADIO STATION

When you gain control of your mindset and attitude, your direction of life begins to progress. Let's say you have kids in the backseat and they have access to the radio controls. Even though they are passengers, they have control over what is played up front as well. We often let others have control over our minds. You need to be able to control the radio and not let others change your attitude. Become strong and control the weather in your life.

Growing up, my dad would say, "It's a beautiful sunny day" even when it was raining because he realized that the weather outside should not control the weather inside your mind. For most of my life, I let the outside environment affect my internal environment. If it's snowing and cold outside, why does it need to be the same inside your house? If you keep your windows open, then it will be cold, but if you shut them, the heat will stay inside. Become strong enough in your inner engineering that your outside issues don't bring you down.

"LEARN TO CONTROL THE NEWS FEED OF YOUR LIFE, SO THAT YOU'RE VIEWING THINGS THAT TRULY FULFILL YOU."

KNOWING YOUR GAPS

When you think about the holes or drop-offs in life, these are the places in which we sink in or fall. Often, these gaps can be our own personalities. It has been said that on average we have about seven to ten personalities that show up at certain times in our life based on situations. Some examples of these personalities can be:

- Military

- Wimpy

- Nurture

- Business Manager

- Perfectionist

- Social Butterfly

There are no specific names for these traits, so you can create your own names to describe what you are going through. Some personalities are good, and others need to stop showing up. You can audit them to see which ones you need to dispose of and which ones you should cultivate.

For example, if your military personality is often used with your kids, this may cause them to resent you and make them want to do the opposite of what you say or demand. It also puts fear in them and builds a disconnect where they will not open up to you. You could try being more nurturing and approach them with a loving but stern approach that will gain their attention more. You may have people in your life who walk all over you, and maybe it's because you're wimpy and scared. Maybe you need to become stronger and learn how to communicate with strength but also with grace as well. Learn to be assertive when you need to in life but in the proper way. There are some great personality tests you can take that allow you to discover your tendencies of who you are as an individual.

"WE TAKE TESTS TO LEARN ABOUT EARTH SCIENCE, BUT NEVER TAKE A TEST TO LEARN WHO WE ARE AS AN INDIVIDUAL."

A great book to read is *Personality Plus* by Florence Littauer. She describes four personality temperaments:

- Sanguine (lively, optimistic, carefree)

- Choleric (goal-oriented, focused, likes control)

- Melancholic (love traditions, very orderly, accurate)

- Phlegmatic (people person, loving)

Discover what's under the hood of your body, mind, and soul. See how it operates, what areas you can improve on, and when they show up.

KNOWING YOUR TEMPERATURE

I want you to think about the outdoors where you are right now. Is it cold or hot outside? If you're indoors, most likely there is a thermostat that controls the temperature. But when you look outside, you don't see a thermostat. If the doors and windows are closed, then the outside temperature should not affect the inside temperature. But if it's cold outside and the door is open, most likely the heat will turn on to get the room back to the correct temperature.

Our attitude is like a thermostat; it's only affected if we let something from outside of us come inside to change it. We need to set the right temperature in our life and not be so controlled by outside weather or people. We need to regulate our life properly to make sure our internal regulator doesn't get too cool and stays at a warm enough temperature to keep us moving.

"IN LIFE, WE SOMETIMES DRIVE WITH OUR WINDOWS OPEN WHEN IT'S COLD OUTSIDE, AND THEN COMPLAIN AND WONDER WHY IT'S NOT WARM INSIDE."

A comfortable temperature in your room or car may be nice, but a comfortable temp in your life will never motivate you to do more. Your internal thermostat is your identity and your expectations of what you believe you should be and do. If it's cold, then you need to change your proximity to get hot. There are four things that will shift your temperature:

1. Power of association

2. Behave differently and break your patterns; shock your system

3. Stop doing what is no longer needed

4. Stop being stuck in the same story.

Let me tell you a story about a time I was afraid of heights. It was probably five years ago, and I really didn't like heights. I woke up one day and said enough was enough; I needed to get over this. I went on a trip to Costa Rica that spring with some friends, and we decided to do zip lining. Now, this is not basic zip lining, this is 2,000 feet in the air over cliffs going across the jungle nine times. The funniest thing was going up the mountain in this crappy little truck that I thought was going to die on the way up. You get to the top, and they give you one glove and say it's the brake to stop. We went down the first line, and man, that was crazy and scary! I then had to go down eight more lines to make it back to base. Plus, as you zip through the jungle, you have monkeys throwing stuff at you because we are in their home.

A few months later, I was sitting at my parents' house, and we were talking about my brother's birthday and what he wanted to do. Out of nowhere, he mentions he wants to dive out of a plane. Twelve hours later, the next morning, we were watching a course about diving out of a plane with this old guy with a beard saying you could die doing this. The next thing you know, we're 10,000 feet up in this small plane, and the door opens. I have never been on a plane with an open door before. We looked down, and then we jumped. Once you're gliding, it's awesome until you realize you're praying for the parachute to work when you see your friend's house and pool from up above.

Then, three months later, my dad's friend invites me to 432 Park Avenue on a beautiful September morning to a building 82 stories high that's still under construction. We get to the building site, and we have to take a construction elevator to the top that's a little more than a metal cage going up the outside of the building. The guys knew I was scared, so they acted like they were panicked and said, "Did you feel that?"

I said, "Dude, please don't do that again!" We got near the top, and we're on the 76th floor, which still has no windows. It's all open, and we started walking up the stairs that are concrete, then wood, then we see a ladder. The worker starts climbing, and I said, "Where are we going?"

He said, "To the top!" I was like, *Please God be up here with me!* We go up two ladders and get to the top, and I see blue sky above me. We get up to the 80th floor and the floor is all wood with no concrete. But man, the view was so amazing. Seeing NYC from that height was incredible. It was so scary but so worth it. In these three stories:

1. I was around people who pushed me through with the power of association.

2. I didn't think, I just committed and did it. I broke my pattern.

3. Stopped just sitting around and thinking and instead took action.

4. I was no longer afraid of heights anymore because it was an old story that I had moved past.

We often have fear that stops us and seems impossible to overcome, but in reality, it's just a paper-thin wall. On the other side of this wall are amazing experiences, but many never find out because they never push through to see what's beyond.

"YOUR ATTITUDE IS LIKE A CITY; IT'S ALWAYS UNDER CONSTRUCTION TO BECOME BETTER."

UPGRADING OUR SOFTWARE

Personal growth is doing activities that improve our awareness and identity, which allows us to develop talents and potential that enhances our quality of life. It's a never-ending journey that allows us to become the best at our future role, whether it's as a mentor, parent, teacher, manager, or just a great person for society. It helps you with your life identity that sometimes we are often confused about. I know I have been. We try to operate on software that is old and doesn't work as well. Have you ever tried to use an old computer and you can't believe how slow and outdated it is? If you don't take the time and money to invest in upgrading your mind and soul, you will operate on a system that is out of date or perhaps even expired.

"WE UPDATE OUR PHONES BUT NEVER UPDATE OUR MINDS OR LIFE."

BOXES IN LIFE

There was a story about a man that was living in a box with his family and friends. Afraid to leave his family, he stayed in that box for years! There were no doors or windows, but one day he saw a light coming through. It was a little opening that he could barely get through. So, when his family was sleeping, he went out to go explore. He ended up finding a boat and started sailing. A couple of months later, he hit land, which was the Land of America, a new box that was bigger and untouched. His name was Christopher Columbus, and he broke through the small box he was born in and sought that bigger box where others could come and live in. You will not succeed in the same ZIP code you grew up in, and this story is a great example of that.

It's like once you fly first class, flying regular is never the same. You will never forget what you can experience. Once you get that taste of something bigger and better, it stays with you. You may forget someone's name, but you will never forget what you see. Learn to change the boxes in your life and upgrade them so you can see different parts of the world that you have never seen before.

Recently, I was in Vermont skiing again (as you can see, I love the mountain life) and we stayed in this beautiful home surrounded by woods and nature with mountain views. We went upstairs trying to look for the third bedroom that they had advertised, but we couldn't find it. They said something about a bookshelf secret door. We tried moving it and then saw the door slide to the right, revealing a secret passageway. Two steps went up into the master bedroom. Our talents are often hidden behind secret doors. Remember, the doors that you don't open in life—because you are afraid or others say you shouldn't—are doors that remain closed.

City of Dreams

They say a skyline all started with dreams,
People willing to work and make it solid with
    every beam,
You think of life as a skyline at times,
Built piece by piece with special signs,
Every building was once a thought,
That someone created and it was caught,
Into their mind so that others will see,

Their vision become reality which is key,
Too many dreams die below ground,
Because people are afraid to make a sound,
In this game we call life you see,
It's those that have courage to be,
Something that others are not willing to do,
You decided to be different and
No one may have believed or ever knew,
Stay steady along this journey you are living,
Just make sure you remain faithful and giving,
Every day that skyline will change a little,
Just make sure you stay in the middle,
Of your beliefs and values without knocking
    others down,
Because a great building in life always has others
To share & be around.

—Steven Mazzurco, April 2019 in NYC

"YOU CAN NEVER CROSS THE OCEAN UNLESS
YOU HAVE THE COURAGE TO LOSE SIGHT
OF THE SHORE."

PERSPECTIVE AND GRATITUDE

One day you are driving, and a rock hits your windshield, and it starts to crack. You get upset about it. A short while later, you are in Africa to spend time with a tribe that has no electricity in town. You start talking to the leader about what happened to your windshield, and he looks at you with confusion. He says that while you're worried about your windshield, they are concerned about having enough food and water for their families to stay alive. They also have lions prowling around their home, ready to attack their children.

Our first-world problems seem silly in comparison to the real problems the rest of the world deals with. I remember a couple of months ago being upset about certain things in life while I was skiing. I had just come down the mountain, and while I was in line after a tough run down the mountain, I saw a gentleman who had no legs going up the lift. My attitude changed very quickly. While many people focus on the negative in their lives, this man with no legs looked at the positive and took away the excuse that he couldn't ski. We sometimes get so consumed with our issues and don't look at the many things we have to be thankful for. We get depressed and blame other people or circumstances for why things aren't going our way, but it's really all a matter of perspective. Stop being the victim and start being the victor of your attitude and life. If you had 31 days to live, would the situation that is bothering you really matter? It is amazing how limited time changes our whole perspective of life's issues that really are nothing compared to life itself.

"FALLING INTO A RIVER DOES NOT DROWN YOU,
STAYING IN THE RIVER DOES."
—PAULO COELHO

PEACE

One of the reasons we love the water or woods is because of the peace we hear and see. Our life sometimes goes so fast that we don't even take the time to look around us. The earth has an annual trip around the sun but so does your life. Does the earth move around you or do you move around the earth? The enlightened person travels without moving because, when they go outside, they see life and nature moving even when they are still. But you will never know that until you find true peace. We might feel anxiety when we are trying to run so fast that we forget to listen to our own bodies. Try this right now: Take ten long, deep breaths and listen to what is around you for two minutes. Close your eyes, and you will realize that you weren't moving, but the earth was moving around you.

"BECOME THE ARCHITECT OF YOUR OWN PEACE."

WHAT'S YOUR GIFT?

The moment you figure out your gift in life, your whole world will change. Your talents are what come naturally to you. When you find your true gift, you won't have issues waking up in life. God will give you room to grow because you are using what you always had inside of you. Sometimes, we don't get our internal thermostat warm enough for us to move forward the way we can. Many of you reading this have gifts that you have been afraid to try using because you're afraid of being judged. Stop that! Eventually, you will judge yourself for never trying to make it happen. Our gift to ourselves can become a gift to others to make an impact. We sometimes let others dictate what we are. I want you to think of this saying by Charles Sooney that is simple but powerful:

"I AM WHO I THINK YOU THINK I AM."

Authorship is how we present ourselves to the world. You can construct how others perceive you based on only an online image. True authentic self is often lost. We come to be and are formed from the interactions of other people. We model what we think they think of us, and that's what we become. Self is not a solid thing when others are what make it solid. That is why I say that in today's world we have an online image and an offline image. We forget to build our offline image and at times have others building our image for us based on what society feels we are or should be. This is a dangerous spot to be in, and you must create your own identity and also seek out your true gifts so that who you become is authentic and real.

"LEARN TO UPDATE YOUR SCRIPT SO YOU CAN CHOOSE WHICH LEADING CHARACTER YOU REALLY WANT TO BE. YOU CANNOT HAVE A NEW STORY WITH AN OLD IDENTITY."

In the movie *A Star Is Born*, Lady Gaga and Bradley Cooper play great roles in a powerful, heartfelt movie. One of the things I took away, which I later found out was what Bradley Cooper actually said to Lady Gaga, which was, "I don't want you wearing makeup. Stop trying to cover what is under that; be the real you." That was powerful and true. We cover up our identities, but those things that make us different make us unique and special. We often cover up who we are, and we never get to really see the true gifts God gave us.

To see an actor turn singer or a singer turn actor is amazing because it shows we all have hidden gifts that need to be unmasked to see them. Don't try to be perfect; just be you. No one relates to perfection. That's why Oprah or the Beatles were so popular because they were just real and showed up as who they truly were. We need to ask ourselves, *If I lost this beauty tomorrow or these muscles or this lifestyle, what would be left of me?* Sometimes, the petty things in life that we think are what makes us who we are, are not our gifts at all.

"YOU NEED TO IDENTIFY AND UNDERSTAND YOUR GIFT TO THE WORLD. ONCE YOU DISCOVER THAT, YOU START TO CURE THE WORLD WITH THE LIFE MEDICINE (GIFT) YOU GIVE BACK TO PEOPLE. YOUR GIFT FROM THE UNIVERSE IS LIFE, AND WHAT YOU DO WITH THIS LIFE IS YOUR GIFT BACK TO THE WORLD."

THE JOURNEY

Personal growth is a journey of discovering the machine, which is you, and seeing how it works and operates. You meet a lot of people that are in surviving mentality, and at the end of the day, you can't live a new life with the same old information. Personal growth is growth that is for you personally, but it affects everyone. It's building your home properly so that people will be attracted or inspired by who you are or are becoming. The first person who needs to be inspired is you. Self-worth is everything. We allow society's opinions to defeat our self-worth, and that's unfortunate.

People may force you to become something you're not. Most people mean well, but at times they may put limits on us and let us lose track of our identity. God gave you gifts and made you perfect how you are. Can we improve on those gifts? Of course. When you buy a home, you don't usually leave the home the way it is. You paint and add rugs, furniture, and do landscaping. But if you add too many things, you go broke or the home becomes too cluttered. I'm sure many of you go back to your parent's house where you grew up and you see things there from the 70s and your parents won't throw away anything. It's like videos that were recorded on VHS but won't ever be watched again. Growing up, my dad had one of those big video cameras that recorded every at-bat of mine while playing baseball. I'm convinced he developed big biceps because the camera was so big and heavy.

If we don't personally grow and find our identity, we become confused about who we are. Growing personally and discovering yourself is key. Like I always say, life is an open-book test, but you first need to open up the book. Audios, reading, travel, and mentors are a big part of your personal growth. It's little pieces at a time that eventually builds a home that develops memories and a great environment that we enjoy.

True growth is about empowering yourself to feel worthy enough to go out in the world to kick butt. My junior year in college is where my life really shifted because that was where I got into business and started to get mentored, but also my baseball career started to move forward. In my sophomore year at Stony Brook, I batted .240 and was about to get released from the college. I was a liability not an asset to the team. I was blessed to get one more chance that September for fall baseball to prove to my coaches and team that I deserved to be there.

That summer, I read more books than ever and worked out harder on my craft and skill. My personal growth and mental attitude changed. I read a book called *Mental Toughness* that changed my mindset on the game of baseball. It taught me the mentality of the greats in baseball of how they studied and played the game to operate at a high level. I went from about to be released from the team to 11 months later batting .369 and winning a championship and MVP to head to college regionals. Life can shift quickly depending on your mindset. You can drive a car for a while, but if you don't have a GPS, you may never reach your destination.

"YOUR BIGGEST DISAPPOINTMENT IN LIFE WILL
SOMETIMES BE YOUR BIGGEST RESCUE."

As you grow, you will experience failure along the way. I think you must look at failure as a successful discovery of something that did not work. Those times will allow you to discover more things about yourself and those around you and make your journey enjoyable. What we fear most is what we most need to do.

Knowing others is Intelligence.
Knowing yourself is true wisdom.
Mastering others is strength.
Mastering yourself is true power.

—Lao Tzu

GRATEFUL AND PERSPECTIVE

I'll finish this section with two stories. As I was wrapping up this chapter, my view was of my computer, a cup of tea, a glossy white table, and a window overlooking small mountain hills in my backyard with a light covering of snow. I saw geese gliding across the sky above me. I think every day God gives us signs to make us realize how special life is. Just think of what it takes for those birds to fly together that high and make a V formation to work and be stronger together. I noticed they take turns for who's in the front to reduce the wind that hits them and it makes it easier for those in the back to fly. Learn from life and nature because it will give you signs of how to live, be grateful, and work together. Don't compete against one another but complete each other, just like the geese do as a team along their journey.

I think we need to appreciate the length but also the depth of life. We sometimes look at the length of all of those years, but we forget to look at the depth of those special moments we have with those we love. Be more present and just breathe.

Every time I look at nature, I'm amazed by how it operates. What I love about kids is that they are curious and seek out fun, but as we grow older, we lose that. Continue to live that curious and fun life, and I promise you will never grow old. I have seen it with my own parents who are young at heart with amazing energy.

The last story is about my mother who recently texted me this. It touched my heart because she is truly a beautiful person inside and out. She is strong-minded with a great personal growth mindset, and she has always been there for us. This is what she sent me, and I wanted to share it with all of you to wrap this chapter up. Enjoy.

From my mom in a text message:

This is my story:

Life is not perfect, and no matter what age you are, there will always be setbacks to face! When this happens, only YOU can face these setbacks and get back on track with yourself!

I suffered a fall a couple of years ago and dislocated my shoulder! Shoulder was reset and went for physical therapy and started to feel a little better. However, in the past year have been experiencing severe pain when lifting the arm so went back to see my orthopedic doctor! Had an MRI done and was told my rotator cuff is severely damaged because of the fall and severe arthritis set in and have several torn tendons that can never turn back into muscle!

At that moment flashes of my life at age 69 went through me as being disabled in my golden years! Memories of my father flashed by because he too had a dislocated shoulder from slipping on a banana peel and never recovered and his quality of life declined because he was unable to use his arm!

At that moment thinking of my father weakened my mind and I started tearing up and feeling sorry for myself and saying, "Why me?"

My doctor gave me 2 options:

Get a steroid shot as needed and do physical therapy or schedule surgery for a rotator cuff replacement.

Surgery was out of the question for me, so I chose to be positive and do physical therapy and get a steroid shot as needed.

I will choose to continue going to the gym and getting my lower body in shape and swimming. Hopefully, physical therapy will stimulate whatever muscles and tendons I have left, but at least I will be in control of my health and quality of life!

I WILL NOT LET THIS SETBACK DEFEAT ME!

We are in control of our well-being at all times! No one can do it for you!

The moral of my story is to help others who may feel defeated and to shift your mind into gear and do something about it instead of feeling sorry and helpless!

Life is precious! Appreciate everything and everyone around you every day!

Love, Mom

QUIZ

Rate this Rock for yourself on a scale from 1–10.

_____

_____

What was your top take-away from this chapter?

_____

_____

What gaps do you have in this Rock?

_____

_____

What is your game plan and action to fix these gaps?

_____

_____

THE 7 ROCKS OF LIFE

OVERALL QUIZ

Which Rocks need the most work in your life. Rate them in order from 1 to 7

_____

_____

Total your Rock Ratings from the end of each chapter. What is your total score? A perfect score is 70.

_____

_____

CONCLUSION

I finish this book with this image and something I wrote in the late summer only two months into my trial of life. I received a gift from someone who gave me an hourglass with sand. It was a beautiful piece, and the sand was my favorite color—blue. After looking at it for months, it spoke to me one day, and I wrote a poem called "Time."

Time

What if your life was like this time glass?

The top part of sand represented your life

Left and the bottom part was the time that passed.

All the good or bad.

The great experiences, trips, relationships, tough times, dreams achieved, people you have helped.

The top part symbolizes the time that is left in your life telling you

Exactly when your day is to come.

THE 7 ROCKS OF LIFE

If you knew that day and physically saw that
time left every day when you woke up how would
you choose to live it?

Would you get hung up with your problems currently?

Would you change your day to day routine?

Would you love more and forgive more?

Would bitterness not really matter?

Imagine you had a certain amount of sand left that
told you your time

Here in this life…What would you do differently?

What things would you change?

How would you go about your days?

How would you treat people?

Life is so precious!

But at the end of the day,

We think we have unlimited time/sand left

To let things bother us and not enjoy this time.

You look at stories of 9/11,

Those people did not know what would happen
that day at work.

The day you wake up and a loved one is gone
out of nowhere.

A mother who is about to give birth but has
a miscarriage

Or an accident happens that was out of your control.

See God gave each one of us a certain
amount of time here.

CONCLUSION

Challenge is we don't know what that time is and
sometimes don't truly value it.

Remember to choose the things that bother you, the
things you do, the people you love. Within this time
you have here, make sure it is spent wisely.

Life....IS precious.

Every day is a blessing to make this world
a better place.

Don't regret things. Learn from them.

Take risks.... that of course are not too dangerous.

Love everyone including your enemies.

Take care of yourself so you look good in heaven.

Be easy to forgive those that maybe hurt you.

The thing that broke around the house...
It's not a big deal, relax.

The guy that cut you off say thank you

His time in life is also running out too

We all are where we are supposed to be based
on our actions

And reactions.

So, make sure you realize and react in a positive
way every day and know that

Time is being lost every day.

So, embrace the moments

With your family

The vacations

The food

THE 7 ROCKS OF LIFE

The holidays

The conversations you have with people.

Life is so precious, but it's what you leave *in* people

Not just *for* people that matters.

People remember what you stood for and lived for.

If you can't control your time stop trying to
control others.

Yes, you can control your health and actions,
but there are things

That you can't control.

When you do try to control just remember
you waste time

On something that won't change.

So today look at life as a gift!

Trust in God's Plan.

Learn not to let money control you so that
you can choose

What you want to do with your time.

You'll see the most rewarding thing you can do is
creating bonds or giving back

With people you love in places you'll never forget.

Time is like water in the desert. It may be there
for a while but eventually

It will dry up.

So, take advantage of the time you have today.

–Steven Mazzurco

CONCLUSION

With everything I was going through, I realized the true currency of life is time. Seven months ago, I hit rock bottom in my life. Seven months later, I wrote a book and started a podcast, clothing brand, vlog/blog, new website, and charity. I am still doing business coaching through it all, which I truly love. The only thing missing is maybe an album because I do love singing. Hey, you never know! Your life can shift quickly, but it is a choice and getting these Seven areas right in life keeps me on track!

From the bottom of my heart, it means so much to me that you took the time to read this book, especially if you got all the way to the end. Sorry there were no Cliff Notes. Thank you for being part of this SeVen RoCk LiFe journey. The reason why the VCF is capitalized, is because it stands for three things:

Victorious in life
Contributor to society
Fun along journey

I want you to be victorious in all areas of your life. You deserve it and have what it takes. Always remember that it's a choice. When you become victorious, it's your duty to give back to others and the universe. The universe gives to us every day, such as water, oxygen, soil, etc. For us to be in alignment with the universe, we must also be giving and contributing.

And, of course, have fun along the journey. Like I have spoken about before, kids seek out two things in life: adventure and fun. That's why we enjoy them so much. As we get older, we stop seeking those things out. So be adventurous and have fun every day; that's what the SeVen RoCk LiFe is all about. The podcast we have for our brand is called Seven Rock Life on iTunes & Spotify, and it is about living all Seven Rocks of Life & *Stories That Inspire With People You Will Admire.* One day, I'd love to have you on the show to share your story to the world of what happened when you implemented the Seven Rocks Of Life along your journey.

I pray these areas of life will encourage you to work on them and share with others to create happiness, peace, and joy in their lives. Every day is a day to add to your life resume to decide to change future for the better or put new things on your life resume to enjoy. The power of life is in your hands with the proper foundation and balance in the seven areas of life.

If you visit StevenMazzurco.com and SevenRockLife.com, you will see videos of Project Impact and ways to support our mission. Subscribe to our newsletter under StevenMazzurco.com/charity to get latest updates with Seven Rock Life and its journey around the world. As a community, we can change lives together, and that's our mission.

- Thank you for caring.

- Thank you for being you.

- Thank you for being a winner and a fighter.

CONCLUSION

You are awesome and deserve only the best! Keep living that SeVen RoCk LiFe! God bless you all!

—Steven Mazzurco
PS: I will always be your friend.

"GOD'S GIFT TO US IS LIFE. OUR GIFT BACK TO GOD IS WHAT WE DO WITH THAT LIFE."

ACKNOWLEDGEMENTS

- God - You were always there for me. At times, I felt I had no one, but I could always count on you being at the dinner table with me. You created this brand; I am just borrowing it from you while I am here in this world.

- Mom and Dad - Thanks for being rocks I could lean on in tough times. My relationship with you both has only gotten stronger. Thanks for staying young, fun, and loving. You truly are phenomenal parents.

- Vinny - My bro! What can I say, man, you truly were there for me when I felt like the whole world was abandoning me. When things got scary and I didn't want to be here, you kept telling me I was important. Thanks for being my ski buddy, roommate, hot tub buddy, and my bro. I truly appreciate you for believing in me and being the light when it was dark.

- Jaclyn and Madison - Proud to call you my sis, Jaclyn. I will never forget our trip driving to Vermont and our special bonding time. Madison

243

is lucky to have a mom that cares so much about her. Thanks for being a great sister and for coming in the backyard that day to talk with me. Moments like that I will never forget and always appreciate it.

- Bryan Lewis - My boy and my brother. Back to back. It all started on a cruise, right? All those calls checking in to see how I was, meant everything to me. Even though we are 3,000 miles away, we are so connected. It's scary yet amazing. I'm proud to have you as a friend.

- Dana Cavalea - Even though we technically only met two times in person, you have played such a huge role in motivating and helping me get this book edited. Thanks for all you do and being someone that gives back and cares. You are a true champion.

- Chris O'Byrne - You are the man! I owe you a few cannolis for all the work and editing you have done. Truly phenomenal work, and I appreciate all your help. You have played such a big role in making this book.

- Patty Morehouse - What can I say; when everyone else left me, you stepped up and came to help me. Every time we had a call, you always taught me something new and helped me make a life shift. Thanks for everything

- Denise Cassino - It has been a true pleasure getting to know you and having you help me get this book out to the world. Your story is inspiring; thank you for being such a help!

- Bill & Tracy Gardell – Thanks for allowing me to work with you as a kid. You allowed me to see what owning a business was all about. You believed in me and helped me envision big dreams. You were great neighbors and had perfect grass which inspired me to have a great lawn as well!

- Mentors/Counselors – Grateful for any advice whether it was for a season of my life or one thing that stood out that impacted me. You can't learn everything from someone but you can learn something from everyone.

- My team - When I was struggling, you all kept me going. You gave me two gifts for my birthday that I will always appreciate: a globe and a yacht. That's something I'll never forget, but what it said on them was key. Impacting lives around the world.

- Friends - Thanks for all who played a role in helping me. With a text, playing golf, saying hello, praying, or just being you and being real! You are all family not just friends. I would do the same for you all! I love you all so much. You played a big part in saving my life when I was down, and I wish only blessings to you all. Keep making a positive impact this world.

RESOURCES

CHAPTER 1

- *The Bible* by God

CHAPTER 2

- "The Differences Between East And West In Terms Of Culture And Education" by Michael Michelini https://www.globalfromasia.com/east-west-differences/

- *Captivating* by John and Stasi Eldredge

- *Wild at Heart: Discovering the Secret of a Man's Soul* by John Eldredge

- *The Ed Mylett Show* Podcast Episode: 310 Pounds to a Nike Athlete - with Charlie Rocket

CHAPTER 3

- https://www.telegraph.co.uk/finance/businessclub/money/11174013/The-history-of-money-from-barter-to-bitcoin.html

- *The Total Money Makeover: A Proven Plan for Financial Fitness* by Dave Ramsey

- Senator Elizabeth Warren popularized the 50/20/30 budget rule in her book, *All Your Worth: The Ultimate Lifetime Money Plan.*

- https://en.wikipedia.org/wiki/Melitta Melitta Bentz 1905 Coffee Maker

- *The Business of the 21st Century* by Kim and Robert Kiyosaki

CHAPTER 4

- https://www.helpguide.org/harvard/vitamins-and-minerals.htm/

- https://www.merckmanuals.com/home/disorders-of-nutrition/overview-of-nutrition/carbohydrates,-proteins,-and-fats

- https://www.betterhelp.com/advice/medication/what-is-the-difference-between-serotonin-and-dopamine/

- https://www.healthline.com/nutrition/10-benefits-of-exercise#section3

- https://www.healthstatus.com/measuring-body-fat-percentage-home/

- https://www.verywellhealth.com/simple-and-complex-carbohydrates-and-diabetes-1087570

Chapter 5

- *The Business of the 21st Century* and *Rich Dad Poor Dad* by Robert Kiyosaki

Chapter 6

- https://www.lifehack.org/articles/productivity/ how-organize-your-life-10-habits-really- organized-people.html

Chapter 7

- *Personality Plus* by Florence Littauer
- https://www.tonyrobbins.com/mind-meaning/ do-you-need-to-feel-significant/

Made in the USA
Middletown, DE
16 June 2019